Better Homes and Gardens®

masonry & concrete Step-by-Step

Meredith® Books
Des Moines, Iowa

TABLE OF CONTENTS

Special PROJECTS 110

Tools AND MATERIALS 126

Solving PROBLEMS 140

INTRODUCTION

When confronted with a masonry job, many people assume they must hire a professional contractor. It must take years of practice, they assume, to lay bricks in a straight line or to install a level, smooth concrete surface. Each year, homeowners across the country pay hundreds or thousands of dollars to professional masons rather than considering taking on the job themselves.

In *Step-by-Step Masonry and Concrete* we don't pretend that jobs are easy when they are not. In fact, there are some jobs, especially finishing concrete slabs, that should be attempted only by a homeowner who has taken the time to learn the skill. Other jobs, such as throwing mortar and laying bricks or concrete blocks, take a good deal of patience and practice to master. But they can be learned, and there are many other projects you, as a homeowner, can tackle without much trouble.

Step-by-Step Masonry and Concrete helps you evaluate what jobs you can take on yourself. You'll find ways of saving money by making repairs and installations yourself. Even if you choose not to do a job yourself, you'll be equipped to manage the job wisely. If you do hire out the job, you'll know whether it has been done right.

Working to code

Although you may be an amateur working on your own house or yard, you have the same responsibilities as a journeyman mason. The foundations you build must be strong enough to support their loads and deep enough so they will not heave upward when the ground freezes and thaws. Walls must be straight, and bricks must be evenly spaced, not only for the sake of appearance, but also so they will last. This means you must use only those techniques and materials that are acceptable to the building codes of your area.

The dimensions and materials given throughout this book work for most situations, but there are important variations. For example, a footing to support a two-story wall needs to be more massive than a footing for a one-story wall. A concrete slab used as a driveway for heavy trucks must be stronger than a slab used as a sidewalk.

Working with your local building department

Always check with your local building department when you are considering adding or changing masonry surfaces or substructures or if you suspect your existing masonry is substandard. Building codes may seem bothersome, but they are designed to ensure your house and other structures are solid and long-lasting. Ignoring codes leads to costly mistakes, weakened structures, and even difficulties in selling your house someday. If you will be building an addition, a new slab, or a patio, check with your building department before proceeding. Neglecting to do so could cause you the expense and trouble of tearing out and redoing your work.

There's no telling what kind of building inspector you will encounter when you apply for your building permit or when you have your site inspected: Some can be helpful, friendly, and flexible; others are real nitpickers. No matter whom you deal with, your work will go better if you follow these guidelines:

- To avoid unnecessary questions about your plans, seek out as much information as possible and incorporate that information into your plan before you take it in for approval. Your building department may have literature explaining requirements for the type of project you have planned.

- Go to your building department with a plan to be approved or amended; don't expect its inspectors to plan the job for you. Present your plan with neatly drawn diagrams and a complete list of the materials you will be using.

- Be sure you understand clearly at what stages of your project you need to have inspections. Do not cover up any work that needs to be inspected.

- Be as courteous as possible. Inspectors often are wary of homeowners because many lack expertise. Show the inspector you are serious about doing things the correct way.

How to use this book

Begin by looking through the first chapter to get ideas and inspiration for the projects you'd like to complete. Also read "Getting to Know Structures" in the first section. This provides an overview of masonry footings, walls, and slabs. The next section, "Working With Concrete," shows you how to plan, form, pour, and finish slabs, footings, and walls. "Laying Patios and Walks" takes you through the basics of constructing a brick, paver, tile, or stone surface, with techniques ranging from laying materials in sand to embedding them in mortar. "Building Masonry Walls" teaches you how to work with mortar and lay bricks, stones, or concrete blocks. Finally, a section on "Special Projects" presents attractive and workable projects to enhance your house and yard.

If you don't have the tools necessary to complete a project, turn to "Tools and Materials" to get an idea of the basic tools you'll need to do projects yourself, and for information that will help you choose the tools you need or want.

When a problem arises, consult the section on "Solving Problems" for help with patching, waterproofing, and anchoring.

Tip boxes

In addition to basic instructions, you'll find plenty of tips throughout this book. For every project, a You'll Need box tells you how long the project will take, what skills are necessary, and what tools you must have before you start. Throughout the book you'll also see Caution boxes that will help you remain safe as you complete a particular project. Other tip boxes are scattered throughout the book, providing practical help to ensure the masonry work you do will be as pleasurable as possible and result in safe, long-lasting improvements to your home and yard.

PRIVATE DINING
A brick patio makes this secluded backyard area highly functional as well as attractive. There's plenty of space for potted flowers and a table and chairs for private dining. Building a brick patio with sand as the foundation is a cost-effective alternative to concrete.

Planning
YOUR MASONRY PROJECT

With the right design, you can combine style and function in a masonry project for your home—a patio that provides an intimate outdoor retreat for relaxing or a fun-loving space for dining and entertaining family and friends; a walkway that welcomes visitors to your front door or ushers them into your garden. Remember, clarifying your vision for a project is just part of the preparation; creating a plan and mapping out a strategy for execution are equally important.

There are several questions to ask yourself as you plan your masonry project. What is the current design theme of your home? What design will best fit with the current landscape of your home? How will you use the space? What is your budget? What type of materials should be used for the project? How much time will it take to complete? Do you need additional help? A little extra time spent researching the answers to these questions, and even consulting with an expert or two, will save you time in the long run.

Get your creative juices flowing by browsing the various design ideas that follow in this chapter; then work through the step-by-step directions for planning your project.

SIMPLIFIED ROMANCE
This circular brick patio within a garden setting serves up romance as well as alfresco dining. Turn to page 62 to learn how to lay a brick patio in sand and page 72 to install a patio on a concrete slab.

OUTDOOR DINING
A privacy fence screens views of neighbors while offering peace and quiet to this patio getaway. The terraced steps expand the visual space of the intimate dining area. When properly installed, brick creates a durable and stable surface for placing outdoor furniture such as this dining set.

COMPATIBLE MATERIALS
This basic brick patio establishes a sense of harmony by drawing from the rich, colorful brick of the home to create an extension perfect for entertaining. See pages 62–65 for directions on installing a brick patio.

DESERT DESIGN
When choosing the materials and design for your patio, consider regional architectural influences. Walled courtyards such as this one dominate the Southwest desert. Terra-cotta walls along the house, around the fountain, and in front of the privacy wall accent this Spanish-influenced design. Large terra-cotta patio pavers visually expand the area and are in keeping with the overall style of the patio and courtyard.

EXPLORE THE POSSIBILITIES

Define a space. Create an intimate enclosure. Extend living space outdoors. Whatever your goals, you can make them reality using masonry and concrete. Whether you are just gathering ideas or are ready to purchase materials for your project, let the ideas in this chapter help you expand your thinking about the possibilities for your home and yard, and then refine your plans as you prepare to begin work on a project.

DEFINE GARDEN SPACES
Stacked-stone walls provide a natural backdrop to garden room enclosures (see pages 82–83 and 84–85). This wall also serves as a retaining wall, creating a higher, level area for plants above the patio area. Soil pockets between the rocks in the wall expand the garden setting by providing a spot for alpine plants to thrive.

MIX MATERIALS FOR VISUAL INTEREST
Defining spaces with distinct personalities makes small areas seem larger. The sweeping curves created by using flagstone for the patio and the walls give a natural feel to this intimate area (see pages 66–67, 85). The straight brick paths add balance and structure (see pages 68–69). Though visual variety adds interest to this small backyard, mixing too many materials can create a disjointed space.

CREATE A PLACE FOR OUTDOOR ENTERTAINING

With a little imagination and some careful planning, a simple backyard can become an extension of living space. Stacked-stone walls surrounding a pond (see pages 82–85) complement the flagstone patio surface (see pages 66–67) in this inviting outdoor room.

TUCK IN A WELCOME RETREAT

Even a small yard can benefit from a quaint patio or walkway. This courtyard is an inviting destination thanks to the brick patio that defines a sitting area and makes the garden beds easily accessible.

INTIMATE TRAVELS

A walkway is more than a means to move from one location to another without getting mud on your shoes. It should provide a natural and visually pleasing transition. Will your path be a graceful sweeping arch past a majestic tree? Or perhaps a curving, rambling trail that encourages guests to explore a lush garden. In some situations a straight, formal walk that leads directly to a home's main entrance might be the most logical. Consider, too, the materials used to create the transition. Whether you use brick, concrete, stone, or loose materials, you make a statement that accents the surrounding landscape for the traveler.

WALK TO THE GARDEN GATE
A narrow brick path gives the landscape a classic look, and its narrow width suggests an intimate sojourn for a traveler.

NATURAL PATH
The stones in the wall echo this walkway. The brick edging provides a distinct contrast to the stone and a practical surface for lawn work.

AGING GRACEFULLY
This path has aged gracefully, as the owner has allowed the moss to grow up between the bricks, creating a relaxed feeling. The bricks are laid out in a manner that guides you up the steps and into the garden.

MIX MATERIALS
Concrete pavers set in gravel beckon a viewer along this casual, less-traveled path. The use of pavers and gravel softens the formal feel the brick creates.

MATERIAL CHOICES

An abundance of material choices combined with imagination and careful planning can turn an ordinary walkway or backyard patio into a resplendent retreat from the workday or an extravagant dining area for guests. Mixing materials adds the mark of personal taste while blending walkways, patios, and walls into the environment. As you make decisions regarding materials for your project, look to your existing home and landscape for inspiration.

RUGGED COMBINATION
Large 4×4-foot sections of exposed-aggregate concrete paired with slate set in concrete creates an attractive and enduring earth-tone floor.

NATURAL CHOICES
Native to the area, the gravel enclosing the brick allows the patio to blend into the surrounding terrain of this Southwest desert home. Using regional materials is visually pleasing and generally cost effective because they tend to be readily available.

SAFE POOLSIDE SURFACE
The choice of sandstone for this patio enhances the appearance of a pool designed to look like a natural swimming hole. Though certainly not harsh on bare feet, the slightly rough surface of the sandstone is ideal next to a pool, where a smoother surface would become slippery.

COLOR INTEREST
Even when using a fairly standard material such as brick, you have color options that allow you to transform a basic design into an eye-catching patio.

FINISHING TOUCHES

The overall look of a masonry or concrete project is determined by the design, the choice of materials, the construction methods, and any finishing touches added to complement your home and landscape. Special touches can turn a basic project into a showpiece. Take concrete, for example. Its low cost and versatility make it the economical choice for a smooth patio surface. Properly prepared, it will last a lifetime with minimal maintenance. But that doesn't mean you have to settle for a stark, gray surface. Specialty finishes are available to transform concrete from dull to extraordinary. Add color. Stain the surface. Introduce a variety of textures. Or stamp the surface while wet to mimic the appearance of brick or stone.

Consider, too, details that you might incorporate into your project. Embellish a wall with decorative capstones or a stone veneer. Add glamour to a standard brick patio by bordering it with stone, or use bricks of different colors to create a pattern. See page 60 for information about choosing a pattern.

>

STONE FACE
Stone veneer sets a rustic though stylish look for this home. The rounded-granite river-rock veneer elevates the appearance of what was an ordinary concrete-block foundation.

<

HEART OF STONE
Stones carefully placed in the shape of a heart offer a touch of romance and add color, texture, and life to this gardens' concrete edge. You can purchase stone pebbles of varying shapes and colors at a local nursery or home center, or gather them from the banks of a nearby lake or river.

ON EDGE
Even a simple finishing touch such as edging a walkway with a contrasting material, as shown here, can be enough to lend an element of style to your project.

MIXING TEXTURES AND MATERIALS
This patio features a washed aggregate surface that has been divided into squares by borders of stone set into concrete.

Garage floors

To withstand the weight of cars and small trucks, a garage floor slab should be at least 4 inches thick. It should be strengthened with reinforcing wire mesh and poured on top of at least 4 inches of solidly compacted gravel or sand.

A footing running around the perimeter of the slab adds extra support for the garage walls. It can be shallow if there is no significant frost danger in your area or if local building codes permit a "floating" slab—one that can rise or fall an inch or so with frost heave. Otherwise, the footing should extend below the frost line. Anchor bolts in the footing allow you to firmly attach the bottom plate of the wall framing.

To handle condensation, blown-in rain or snow, and moisture from vehicles, the slab should slope toward the floor drain or garage door at a rate of ¼ inch per foot.

Footings

Before building a masonry wall, you must pour a solid footing to supply rigid support for the wall. (The exception is a dry stone wall, which has no mortar joints.) How extensive the footing is depends on how much weight it will carry. For a low garden wall you need only a small pad. A tall masonry or concrete wall, however, requires a substantial footing that extends below the frost line.

To support posts for a deck, gazebo, or similar project, you need to set post footings below the frost line or your structure will move up and down with the changing seasons. In warm regions you need only to dig holes and pour in the concrete footings. In colder climates insert cylindrical concrete tube forms into the holes before pouring the concrete.

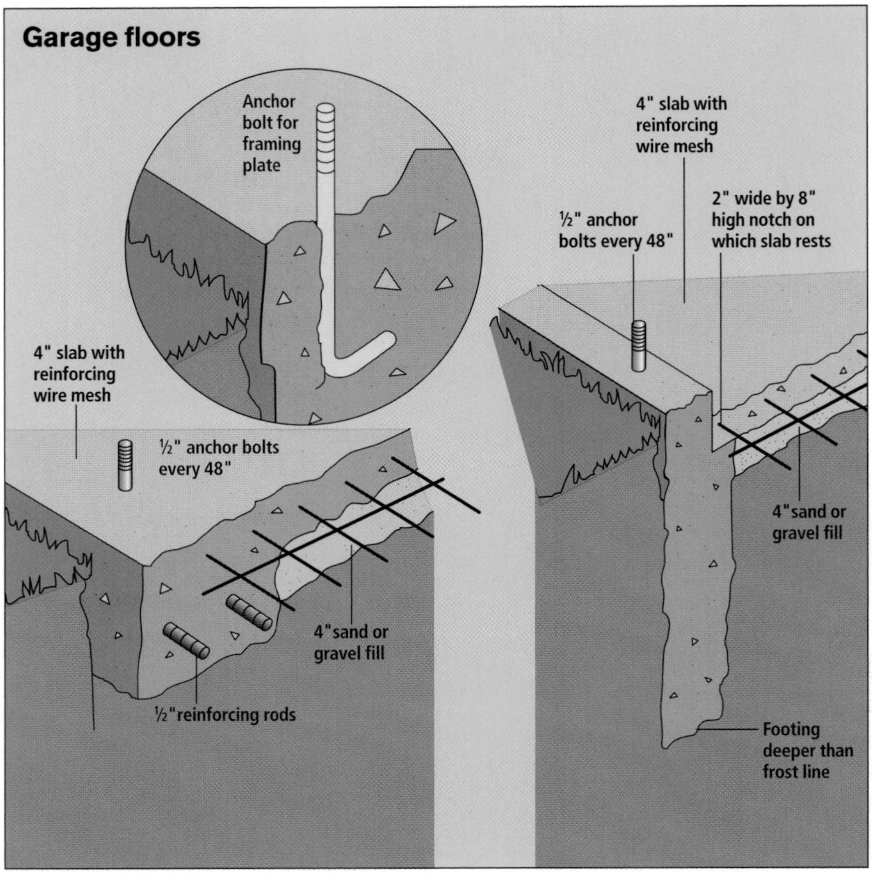

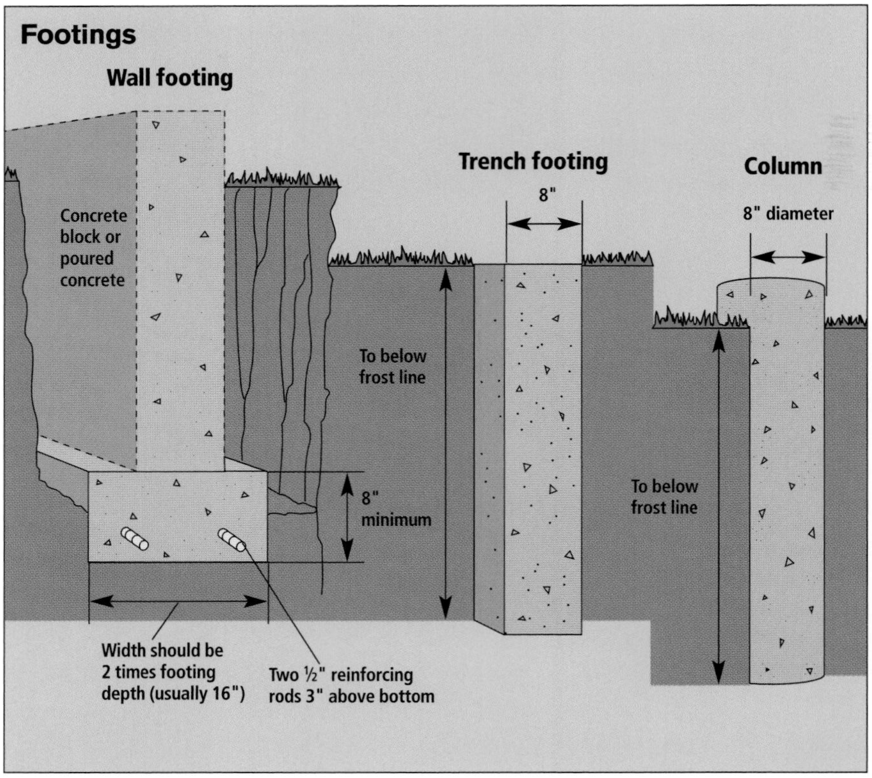

Patio surfaces

If you want to lay a patio of bricks, concrete pavers, or tiles that are ¾ inch or more thick, the most common way is to set them in a bed of sand that rests on a stable surface. If your soil is stable, 2–4 inches of sand alone may be enough of a base. But to ensure that your patio does not settle unevenly, excavate deeper and start with a bed of gravel. Either way, it is important to thoroughly tamp down both the soil and the substrate, using a vibrating tamper that you can rent. Once the sand is level, install the finishing material and fill in the joints between the bricks or pavers with fine sand (see pages 56–65).

Other techniques can be used for patio construction. You can set tiles designed for outdoor use in mortar on a solid concrete base or set flagstone directly on firmly tamped soil (see pages 66–67 and 74–75).

Below-grade walls

To hold back the weight of soil, a wall built below grade must be strong. But even the strongest wall cannot withstand the hydraulic pressure that builds up when soil becomes saturated with rainwater. So, in addition to being built solidly, the wall must have a way for water to escape. Weep holes, small in diameter and spaced 4–10 feet apart, allow water to come through the wall. Or, in the case of a foundation wall, you can direct water to one or both sides of a wall. The most common way to do this is with perforated drainpipe set in a bed of gravel and sloped slightly.

A landscaping retaining wall commonly is battered, that is, sloped toward the soil it retains. This gives the wall strength. Structural walls cannot be battered, so include plenty of steel reinforcement.

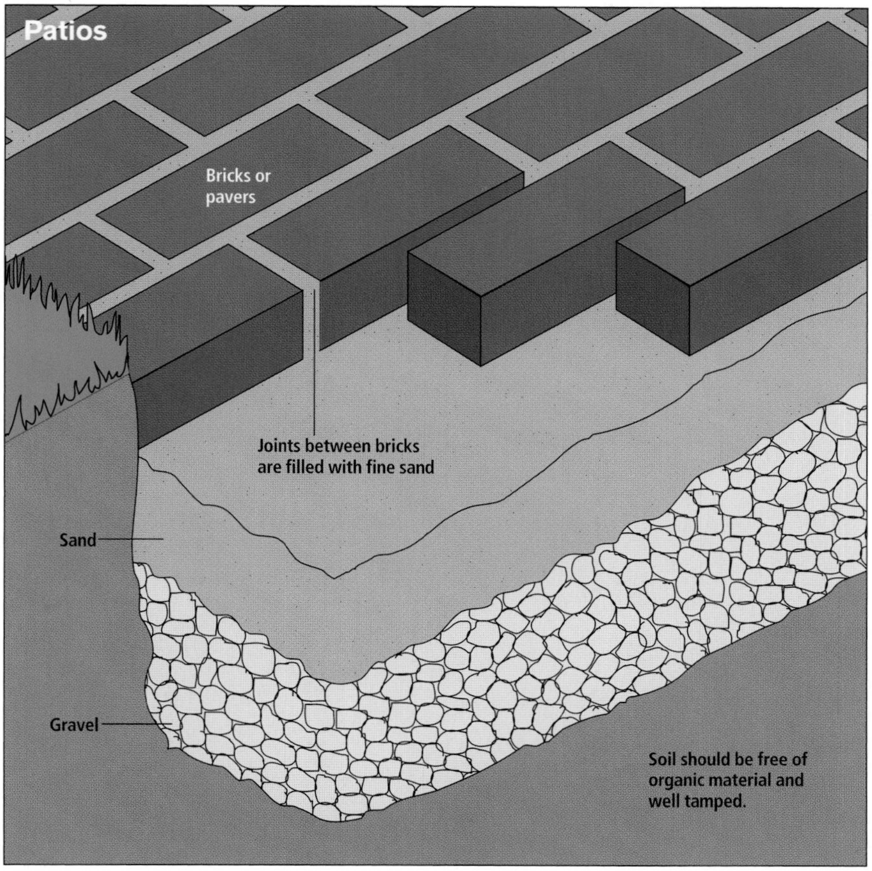

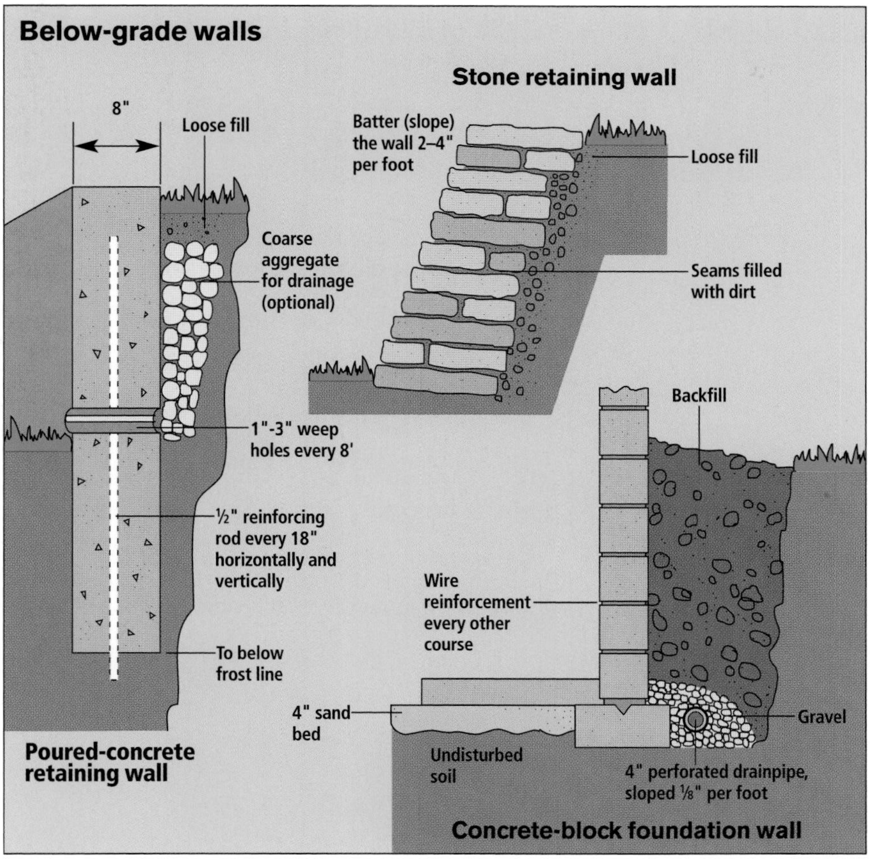

Working WITH CONCRETE

A concrete slab forms the base of many driveways, patios, walkways, and walls. It is the workhorse of materials, providing a solid foundation beneath mortared brick, stone, and tiled surfaces. Concrete slabs can be finished in many ways, depending on the intended use. Options include a variety of colors and textures, such as exposed aggregate or a surface stamped with a pattern. Whether supporting another surface or taking center stage, concrete needs to be properly placed and finished. This section provides ideas for concrete surfaces and takes you through all of the steps necessary to complete a concrete project–from preparing the site for a slab to applying the finishing touches.

SURFACE PREPARATION
Brush the surface of concrete with a stiff-bristle broom to improve traction. You can draw the brush across its width in a straight line, or you can experiment with the pattern of the surface by drawing in wavy lines—the drier the concrete, the finer the brush lines.

ADD COLOR TO CONCRETE
Don't settle for a drab slab patio. By adding color to your design, your imagination is your only limitation. See page 48 for more information and step-by-step instructions for adding color to concrete.

ENHANCE WITH TEXTURE
Textures add natural appeal to concrete. The surface of this exposed-aggregate walkway blends into the garden surroundings. Turn to page 46 to learn how to add custom finishes to concrete.

CONCRETE ART
Color stain applied in simple geometric circles transforms what would have been a drab slab into a contemporary work of art. The first step is to draw the design to scale on graph paper. Then transfer it to the concrete. The choice of colors is up to you—match house trim or extend the palette of an adjacent indoor room outdoors. Color stain is permanent, so select colors carefully and make your final selections outdoors.

AGGREGATE STAIRS
Exposed aggregate blends with the natural and architectural elements of this entryway. Turn to page 32 for information about forming stairways, and to page 24 to learn how to lay out sites for slabs.

SURFACE CHARACTER

Creating a mosaic can be an economical way to add interest to a surface. The use of crescent-shaped casts and stones placed in concrete make strolling along this walkway an elegant and interesting experience.

CLASSIC CONCRETE

Sometimes you want the patio surface itself to take a backseat to other amenities. For this simple yet classic concrete patio, two similar muted brown stains were selected to accent the landscape. Transitions are defined with geometric concrete finish edging.

PLANNING DRIVEWAYS AND WALKS

Walkways and driveways should be both practical and good-looking. Begin your design process by determining the natural routes people take to doors and any high-use areas; you don't want to build a walk that will be bypassed in favor of walking on the lawn. Basic concrete is a plain material, so use it as a frame to outline your lot. Add variety by combining other paving materials with concrete.

Once you have a general plan, visit your building department to find out about zoning regulations and building codes, which typically dictate the dimensions and type of concrete you must use for footings and slabs. They describe how much and what type of metal reinforcement to use and if you need a sand or gravel base under the material. Building codes also spell out setbacks—how close to your property line you may build. Once your plans are approved, you can get a building permit. Plan the work schedule so you will be ready for each inspection.

CAUTION

WATCH UNDERGROUND LINES

Avoid placing structures over underground septic systems and gas, water, electric, and telephone lines. Locate all underground utilities on your property. You may have to call each separate utility company to locate each line. Find out how deep the lines are buried and if your project might harm them. If lines need to be moved, you probably will not be able to do it yourself—utility companies generally own their lines up to the point where they enter your house.

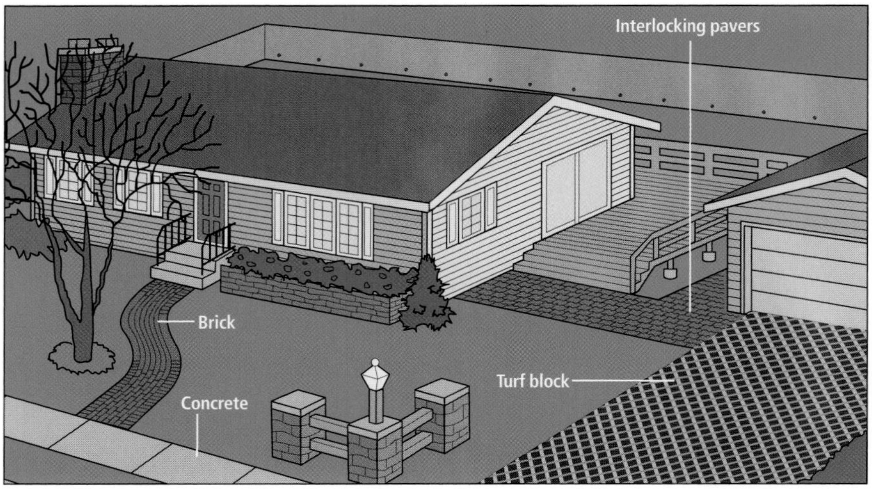

MAKE A TOTAL PLAN.

Planning starts with knowing what you want. Short of hiring an architect, the best way to get ideas is to drive around town and look at other people's drives and walkways.

Use concrete in places where you need solid strength. Large concrete slabs can pose drainage problems, so you may need to install a drain in the middle of the slab, make sure the slab drains into the street, or provide drainage around the edge of slab (see page 24).

For patios and walkways, you usually can install a surfacing material, such as bricks, pavers, or loose material, for about the same price as a concrete slab. If built well, many such surfaces hold up as long as concrete.

PLAN A PATIO SLAB.

Locate a patio slab away from large trees whose roots may crack the concrete. You may need to remove roots as you grade the excavation and before you add the sand or gravel base. Slabs collect a lot of precipitation, so slope the slab away from the house. It should be no closer than 1 inch below a doorsill or threshold. Because concrete does not flex without cracking, you'll need to add reinforcing mesh. Control joints allow the slab to flex without creating unsightly cracks. Expansion joints provide a buffer between the house foundation and the slab. Select a finish (see pages 44–47) and plan on having an experienced finisher on hand.

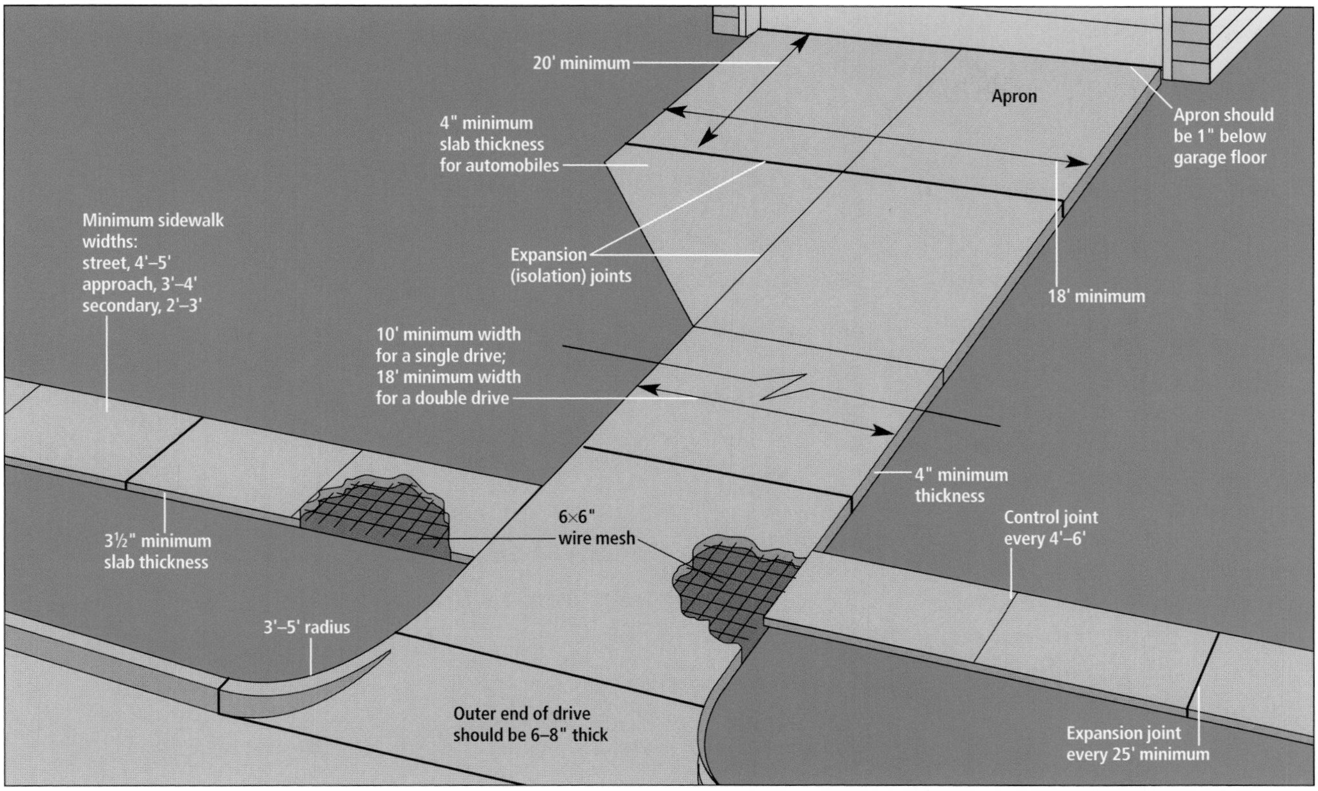

PLAN DRIVEWAYS AND WALKS.

Whenever possible, slope a driveway toward the street and make sure water entering the street can drain away easily. If you cannot do this, slope or crown the driveway slightly so water can drain to the edges, or plan for a drain in the middle of the slab.

The large slab just outside the garage door is called the apron. Make sure it provides enough room for cars to maneuver, especially in the case of a two-car garage. The apron should be 1 inch below the garage floor to keep water out of the garage.

Use expansion strips made of asphalt-impregnated felt wherever new concrete butts up against old concrete or another material. This allows the two slabs to move separately. It is also a good idea to install an expansion joint every 15 feet or so in large slabs.

Cut or strike control joints every 4–6 feet in walks or small slabs (see page 44). These grooves prevent random cracking in concrete slabs.

ADDITIVES FOR CONCRETE

Often, concrete lasts longer if you modify it with an additive. Ask your building inspector and your concrete supplier if they recommend any of the following for your situation.

- If you live in an area subject to severe freezing, consider using air-entrained concrete. This type of concrete is full of tiny bubbles that remain in the concrete after it has set. They enable the concrete to withstand the expansion and contraction that occurs during freeze-thaw cycles. You can order air-entrained concrete delivered in a truck, or you can add an air-entraining agent when you make concrete in a mixer. But you cannot add the agent if you mix concrete by hand. When you add the agent, you will need to cut down on the amount of sand; check the instructions.
- If the weather is cold on the day you pour concrete, consider adding calcium chloride. This will make the concrete set faster, which reduces the danger of cracking due to freezing. Be prepared to work quickly.
- If the weather is hot, it may make sense to order a retarding agent to keep the concrete from setting too quickly.
- In some areas and in some situations, you can eliminate the need for metal reinforcement by ordering fiberglass-reinforced concrete. Compare the price with the cost of wire mesh or reinforcing bar to see if this makes sense for your situation, and check local building codes.

LAYING OUT SITES FOR SLABS

Although concrete is very strong in many respects, it has limited tensile (bending) strength. A slab without a firm, uniform base almost certainly will crack and heave unevenly, leaving you with a difficult repair job. This happens with driveways, for example, where the sand base underneath washes away, allowing the weight of vehicles to crack the slab.

If possible, place concrete slabs on a gravel bed over undisturbed soil—soil that has never been dug up. In many areas, this means digging down until you reach clay. If you must pour a slab on top of recently dug soil (for example, backfill from a foundation), pack the soil by watering it for several days, giving it time to settle. Then compact the earth using a hand tamper for small areas or a rented vibrating tamper for larger areas.

RENT A TRANSIT

For small jobs, using a line level or water level to lay out a level or accurately sloped slab is most likely sufficient, but if you'd like to perform more efficiently and have a lesser chance for human error, consider renting a transit, or better yet, a laser level transit.

Transits are a small telescope-like device that sits on a tripod. By sighting through it, you can determine level points across a distance.

A laser level automatically finds level and shoots a red dot or line up to 200 hundred feet away or more. Combine a laser with a transit and you have the ultimate tool for finding level—ideal for large jobs or if you're working alone. If you rent a transit or laser level transit, be sure that it comes with specific instructions or consult with a professional prior to setting it up.

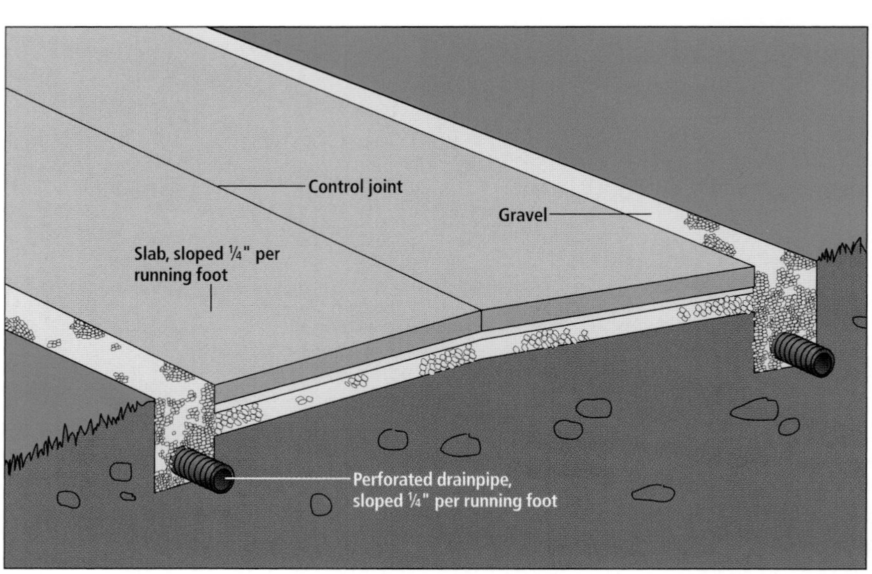

INSTALL PERIMETER DRAINAGE SYSTEMS.

When rain falls on a large concrete slab, the low ends of sloped sections collect water quickly. In many cases, puddling can be solved simply by digging a border and planting flowers or shrubs in a bed covered with wood chips. For more severe problems, dig a trench and fill it with gravel. For even more drainage, dig a trench at least 12 inches deep and install sloping perforated drainpipe in gravel, as shown. Each of these options can be installed after the slab is poured.

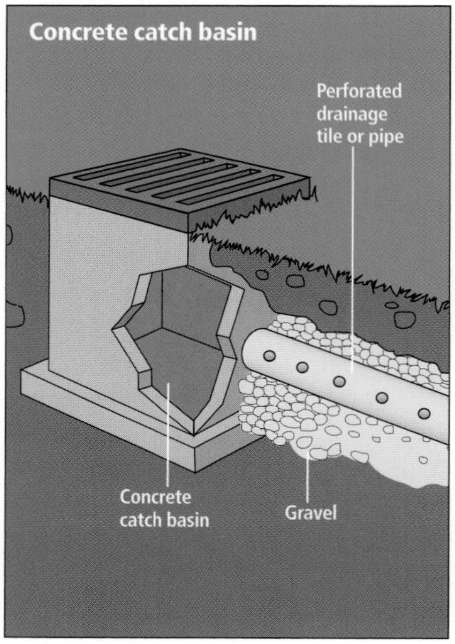

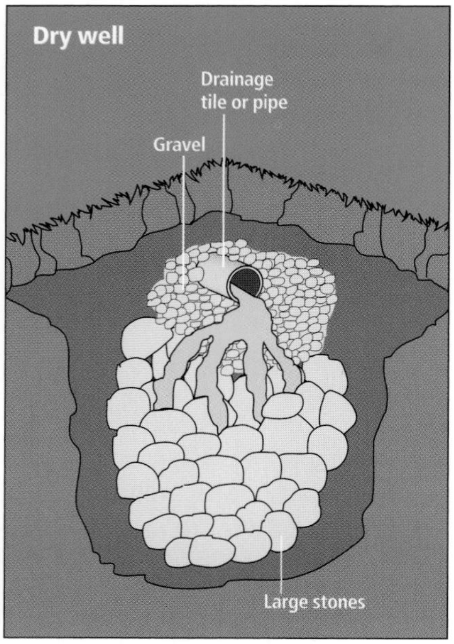

INSTALL A CATCH BASIN AND DRY WELL FOR SEVERE DRAINAGE PROBLEMS.

In large areas where you anticipate water collecting with no place to go, consider sloping the ground toward a catch basin at the center. The water caught there can be piped out into a city sewer system or into a dry well.

A dry well is a large hole filled with stones and topped with a layer of gravel. It holds water until it can percolate into the ground.

CHECK FOR SQUARE USING THE 3-4-5 METHOD.

Drive in a stake at one corner of the slab, such as against the foundation, and attach a mason's line to it. Working from that fixed point, check for square as you drive stakes for the other corners. Use the 3-4-5 method. Measure 3 feet from the stake along one side; mark that point with a stake or tape. Pull the line taut; then measure 4 feet along the line and mark the spot with a piece of tape. Make sure both measurements begin at exactly the same point. Measure between the 3- and 4-foot marks, moving the line until this distance is exactly 5 feet. You'll then have a square corner. Drive a stake and attach the line. If you have room or have a large slab, use multiples of 3-4-5, such as 6-8-10 or 9-12-15.

USE A SQUARE FOR WALKS.

To square one side of a long, narrow slab, such as a walk, use a carpenter's framing square. Square the line from a step, slab, or foundation. Position the second line by measuring off the desired width so the two lines are parallel.

WATER LEVEL

With a water level, you easily can find the same level for two places far from each other, even if you have to turn a corner or two, step down an incline, or climb a couple of stairs.

This simple tool consists of two calibrated plastic tubes attached to a garden hose. Drain spigots and fill spigots let you fill the tubes and hose with water to the desired level. It works on the principle that water seeks its own level.

CHECK BY MEASURING DIAGONALS.

As a final check that the slab perimeter is square, measure from corner to corner in each direction. The two measurements should be the same. Make sure you line up the same edge of the tape measure when you do this. Don't use this method in place of the 3-4-5 method, only as a double-check.

EXCAVATING FOR SLABS

If your soil is soft, your back is strong, and you have plenty of time, you can dig the hole for a small slab by hand (or you can hire young and willing laborers).

For large jobs or in places where the digging is tough, rent a rototiller or skid-steer loader, or hire an excavating contractor.

Remove all organic matter—not only the sod but also roots ½ inch or more in diameter. Many building codes require you to dig down to undisturbed soil (subsoil that has never been dug up).

YOU'LL NEED

TIME: A day for a person to dig 100 square feet 6 inches deep.

SKILLS: Accurate digging, laying out, leveling.

TOOLS: Shovels, spade, small sledgehammer, mason's line, line level, chalk line.

MARK A CURVED LINE.

Where your plan calls for a curve in the slab, lay a charged garden hose (turn on the water with the nozzle shut) in position to mark the slab perimeter. Take into account the width of the stakes and forms. Pour flour or sand over the hose. Lift it up and you'll have an easy-to-follow curved line.

SPARE YOUR BACK AS YOU DIG.

You'll spare yourself pain and fatigue by using your knee, not your back, to push the shovel into the soil. As you dig, position your knee against your lower hand and push forward with your knee. You'll be surprised how much extra force it provides.

1 MARK AND TRENCH THE PERIMETER.

Mark the location of the slab edges by sprinkling flour or sand over the mason's lines strung when you laid out the project (see page 25). Remove the line, but leave the stakes in place. Use the marks as a guide for digging a shallow trench about 1 foot wide. Dig the trench so it extends about 3 inches beyond the outside edge of the slab.

2 MARK SLAB HEIGHT ON THE HOUSE.

If the slab will butt against an existing structure, snap a chalk line on it to establish where the top of the slab will be. Patio surfaces should be about 1 inch below door thresholds to keep rain and snow out of your house. Outdoor slabs should be about 1 inch above the lawn surface. If the slab does not abut the structure, make a mark on one of the corner stakes indicating the top of the slab.

SET LINES AND DRIVE STAKES.

Reattach the mason's lines. Where they meet the house, set them level with the chalk line that marks the slab top. Pull one line taut and level it using a line level (see page 29). Mark the line level on one of the outside corner stakes. Measure down from that mark ¼ inch per running foot of slab (the distance from the house to an outside corner) and make a second mark. Tie the line securely to the second mark. Repeat this procedure on the other side.

Drive in form stakes at a point outside the line at a distance from the line equal to the thickness of the forming lumber. Be sure the tops of the stakes are a little below the level of the line.

CAUTION

When reattaching the mason's lines, be careful not to wrap the lines the wrong way around the stake. If you have any doubts, recheck for square (see page 25).

EXCAVATE THE INTERIOR.

Remove the sod and topsoil to reach the desired depth. If you want to use the sod elsewhere in your yard, undercut it horizontally about 2 inches beneath the surface and cut it into easy-to-handle 8×16-inch sections. Save enough to resod around the edges of the new slab.

If you plan to place sand or gravel beneath the slab, excavate at least 5 inches deep. Check the bottom as you dig by laying a straight 2×4 or 2×6 on edge so its top barely touches the mason's line. If you remove too much soil in some spots, fill them with sand or gravel—not loose soil. Use a flat spade or square shovel to dig the final inch of soil from the bottom and sides of the excavation.

PREPARING SITES FOR WALL FOOTINGS

Because the weight of a concrete slab is distributed over many square feet, it usually does not need footings. Slabs "float" (ride up and down) 1–2 inches as the ground freezes and thaws.

But a footing is required to support most walls (a dry stone wall is one of the few exceptions). A footing spreads the weight so the wall doesn't sink, and it's usually twice the width of the structure it supports. The footing must extend below the frost line to avoid damage from frost heave. Check local codes to see how deep the footing must be.

To do its job without sinking or shifting, a footing must rest on stable, undisturbed soil. A footing beneath a foundation wall also must have adequate drainage to avoid damage from hydraulic pressure (see pages 17 and 145). To make sure you've planned for the demands of your particular climate and soil conditions, consult with your local building department.

FOOTING REQUIREMENTS

- In most situations, a footing 22 inches wide and 12 inches deep, with two pieces of ½-inch reinforcing bar running through it, is strong enough to support a one-story wall. But if the soil in your area is soft, your local building codes may require a larger footing.
- Formed or unformed, a footing must rest on undisturbed soil. If the soil is black, it almost certainly is topsoil and you must dig deeper. In most areas, undisturbed soil will be clay. In some areas, you'll hit bedrock only a few feet below grade. A building inspector should approve pouring directly on top of bedrock, even if you haven't dug below the frost line.

1 INSTALL BATTER BOARDS.

Lay out the job as shown on pages 24–25, driving in stakes to mark the wall's outside corners. Place batter boards about 3 feet beyond these stakes by driving in 1×4 or 2×4 stakes and attaching 3- to 5-foot-long horizontal pieces to them. Fasten with drywall screws. (Nailing will loosen the stakes.)

YOU'LL NEED

TIME: Two days for a medium-size project (12×12 feet).

SKILLS: Excavating, squaring, leveling.

TOOLS: Shovel or digging machinery, screwdriver, mason's line, line level, carpenter's level, plumb bob, hammer.

2 LAY OUT THE SITE.

Attach mason's lines to the batter boards and the house. Transfer the line marking the outside of the wall (inset) to the batter boards by having someone dangle a plumb bob over the outer edge of each perimeter stake while you stretch the mason's line. When the lines intersect over the stake, mark the points where the mason's lines cross the batter boards.

Now that you have marked for the outside of the wall, measure over on the batter board and mark for the inside edge of the footing, the outside edge of the footing, and the outer excavation line. See page 35 for instructions on building forms for wall footings.

3 DIG TRENCH AND LAY OUT FOOTING.

It may not be necessary to build forms for your footings. Depending on your local codes and the nature of your project, digging a trench for the footing may suffice. Check with your local building department.

Digging a hole as big and as deep as needed for a wall footing can be a slow, backbreaking job, so consider hiring an excavator or renting a small backhoe or trench digger. Dig the trench to a depth equal to the top of the footing or to about 3 inches below the top of the footing if you will be building a form (see pages 35–36).

Use a plumb bob to locate the outside corners of the footing. Partially drive in the stakes that line up with the outside edges of your forming lumber. Follow the same procedure to position the form stakes for the inside edge of the footing form.

4 LEVEL TOPS OF STAKES.

If there is a footing on the existing structure, drive in form stakes so the tops of the stakes are at the same level as that footing. Or drive a stake so its top is at the correct depth of the footing top. Then drive the outside corner stakes so they are level with those next to the building. Check for level with a line level or carpenter's level resting on a straight board.

BUILDING FORMS FOR SLABS

Once you pour concrete, your slab will be impossible to change. As wet concrete flows into a form, it fills the niches and faithfully reproduces every detail of the mold you provide.

If you build strong forms that are straight where they should be and curved correctly according to your plan, the final product will look professional. But if you put up forms that bulge, tilt, or have loose-fitting joints, the finished product will have embarrassing flaws for years to come. Take the time to be fussy when building forms. If the formed surfaces will be visible, inspect your forming lumber for knotholes, cracks, and other defects.

Concrete forms must be sturdy, straight, and plumb. If you're in doubt about whether the forms are rigid enough, drive in an extra stake or two and add braces.

YOU'LL NEED

TIME: 4 hours to build forms for a driveway slab with curves.

SKILLS: Measuring and cutting of wood, testing for level and plumb, driving stakes, fastening with nails or screws.

TOOLS: Sledgehammer, circular saw, hammer, carpenter's level, line or water level.

INSTALL STRAIGHT FORMS.

Because most concrete slabs are about 4 inches thick, smooth, straight 2×4s make ideal forming materials. When anchoring the forms, drive two duplex (double-headed) nails through the stakes and into the 2×4s. Place your foot or hold a sledgehammer (below left) against the opposite side of the forms to make nailing easier. Be sure the tops of the forms are level with or above the tops of the stakes, or you will have trouble screeding later (see page 43). Buttress each form with foot-long 1×4, 2×2, or 2×4 stakes every 3–4 feet. Use a string to make sure the forms are straight and level.

FORM A CURVE.

Where your plans call for a curve, substitute 3½-inch-wide strips of ¼-inch hardboard or plywood. For strength, use two or three plies of hardboard. If you use plywood, cut the strips perpendicular to the wood grain of the surface plies so the curved strips will be easier to bend.

Don't try to measure the length of the pieces to be bent. Tack one end temporarily with two 4-penny nails through the thin material and into the stake. Spring the material into the shape you want, mark the point where you'll cut it, and make the cut. Then nail the piece in place.

ADD EXTRA SUPPORT WHERE NEEDED.

Don't skimp on bracing your forms. If the forms collapse in the middle of a concrete pour, it is next to impossible to repair them. Perhaps—on a small, shallow project—you can pound the forms back together, brace them, and shovel the concrete back in place.

When bracing the forms, pay particular attention to places where two forms meet. If the forms butt end to end, drive in stakes to lap the joint. At corners, drive stakes near the end of each form. To strengthen curved forms, drive stakes every 1–2 feet along the outside radius. Fill gaps beneath the forms with rubble or scraps of wood. Resulting irregularities will be buried later.

DIVIDE A LARGE SLAB.

Adding dividers on a large project allows you to pour concrete in manageable amounts at one time. If the dividers will be temporary, use any straight length of lumber. If you plan to leave the dividers in as part of the slab, use redwood or pressure-treated lumber. Two 2×2s sandwich the reinforcing mesh, keeping it at the right level for maximum effectiveness.

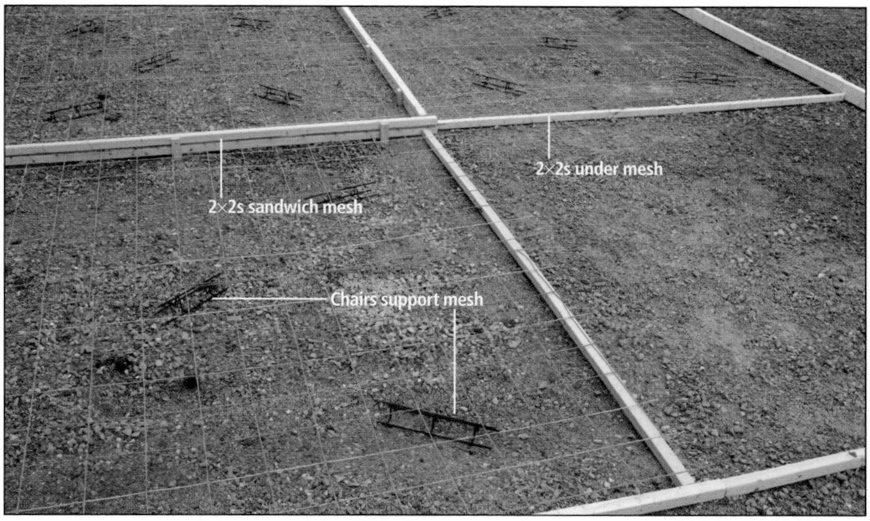

PROTECT PERMANENT DIVIDERS.

Brush on a coat of wood sealer to enhance rot resistance of any wood forms that will remain a permanent part of the slab. Put masking tape on the top surfaces to keep wet concrete from staining the wood and to avoid scratching the forms when you screed. Drive interior stakes 1 inch below the top of the permanent dividers so they will not be visible once the concrete is poured.

FORMING STAIRWAYS

It takes careful planning to build a stairway that is comfortable to walk on. If one step is even an inch or so different from the rest, climbing the stairs will be hazardous.

Each step consists of a horizontal run (tread) and a vertical face (riser). For adults, a riser height of about 7 inches and a tread width of 10–12 inches makes for a stairway that is comfortable and safe.

Steps leading to a house should be at least 3½ feet wide, preferably wider. For flights rising more than 5 feet, a landing with at least a 3-foot run is desirable. However, a landing beneath an exterior doorway should extend 1 foot on each side of the opening and have a run of 5 feet.

YOU'LL NEED

TIME: Two days to figure, form, pour, and finish a small stairway.

SKILLS: Good carpentry skills, ability to figure accurately.

TOOLS: Tape measure, level, hammer, circular saw, framing square, small sledgehammer.

CAUTION

CHECK LOCAL CODES

The building codes for your area may dictate stairway dimensions, such as the size of risers and treads, the relationship between rises and runs, the width and height of steps, the size of landings, and footing requirements. Check with your local building department to ensure your plans conform—before they are set in concrete.

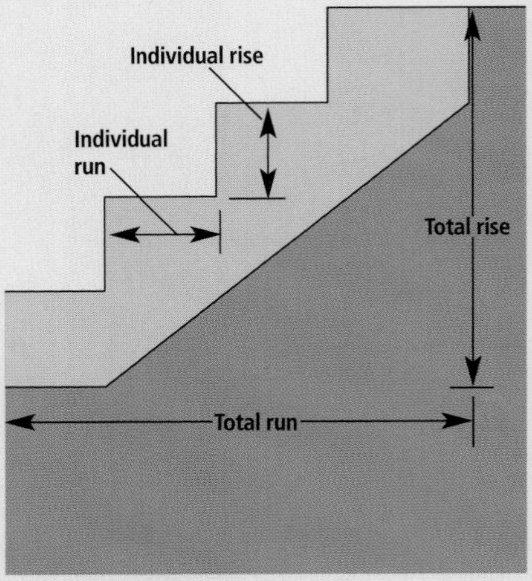

CALCULATE RISE AND RUN.

Total rise is the distance that the stairway rises from the ground to the landing. Total run is the horizontal distance covered by the stairway. Individual rises and runs refer to the height and depth, respectively, of each step. The sum of each run and rise should equal about 18 inches. For example, if you want a series of steps with a gentle rise of 5 inches per step, you should provide treads that are 13 inches deep.

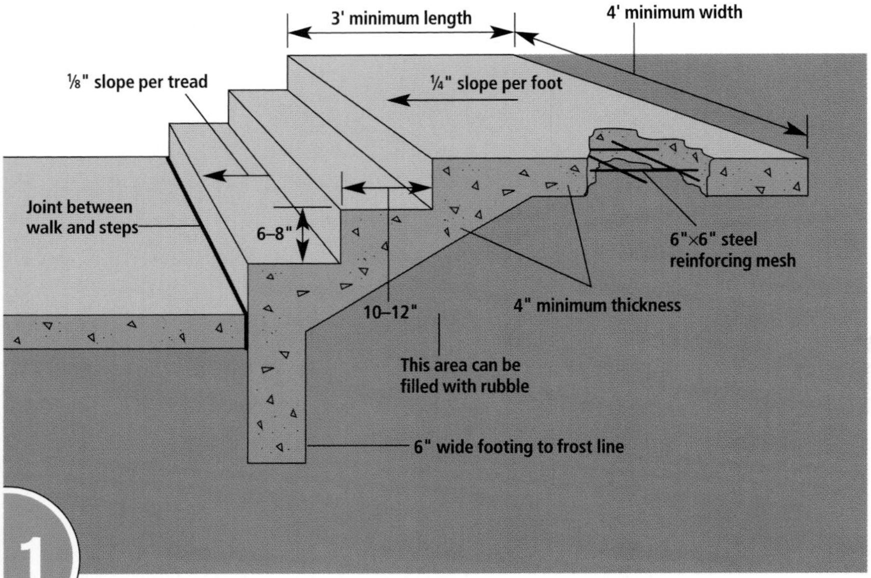

1 PLAN YOUR STAIRWAY.

Measure the total rise and divide by whatever individual rise you plan to use (7 inches is typical). Round off the result to the nearest whole number to get the number of steps. Divide total rise by the number of steps to determine the exact dimension of each individual rise. Decide on how deep you want each tread to be (the individual run). Multiply that run by the number of steps to find the total run and, thus, where the stairway will end.

The footing at the base of the stairway should be 6 inches wide and extend beneath the frost line. (Check your local codes for the exact requirement.) Construct the forms so there is an expansion joint between the stairway and the walk. To keep rain and ice from gathering on the steps, slope each one ¼ inch per running foot for the landing and ⅛ inch per tread.

2 LAY OUT THE SIDE FORMS.

On a sheet of ¾-inch plywood, lay out the side forms by drawing lines showing total rise and total run. When laying out the length of the landing, be sure to allow 1½ inches for the riser forms at the end of the landing. Mark the end of the landing and draw lines establishing the location of the finished treads and risers. For adequate drainage, the landing should slope away from the house at a rate of ¼ inch per running foot.

3 CUT AND POSITION THE FORMS.

Cut both side forms and set them in place at the entry. Use a framing square to make sure they are perpendicular to the building foundation. Check the forms for proper slope and plumb and make sure they are level with each other. Drive supporting stakes into the ground and against the house. Use a small sledgehammer to support the stakes as you nail the forms to them (see inset).

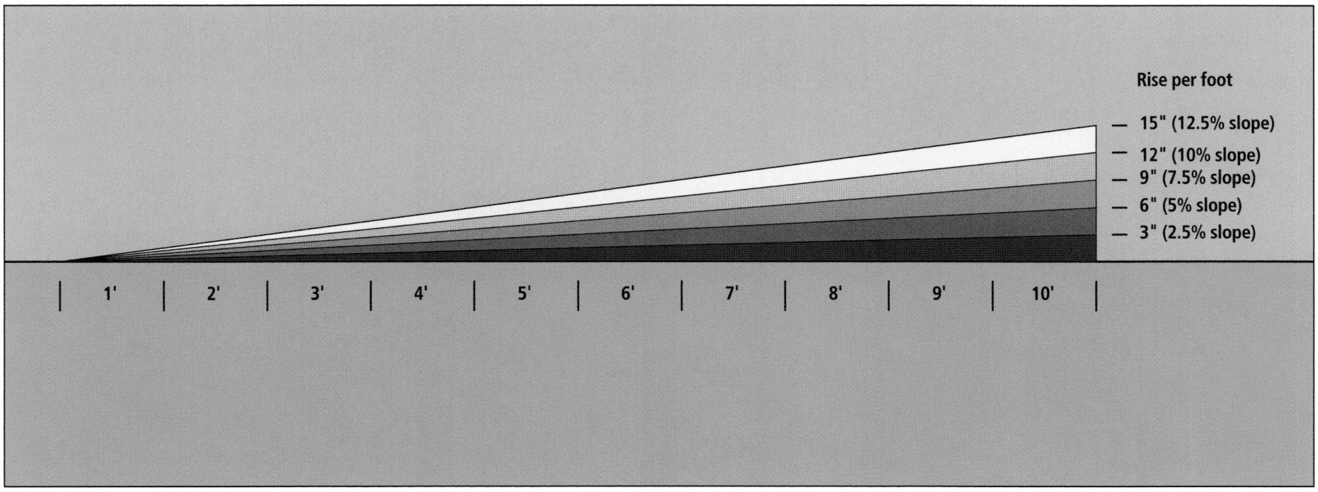

CALCULATE RAMP DIMENSIONS.

Ramps are useful for people in wheelchairs or if you need to move wheeled equipment regularly. Otherwise steps are a better choice; walking down a ramp feels awkward.

To frame a ramp, construct braced forms for the sides. Maintain a constant concrete depth of at least 4 inches, even at the bottom of the ramp. Do not try to feather out the concrete to nothing. For most purposes, it's best if a ramp does not rise more than 1 foot in 10 feet, a 10-percent slope.

Forming stairways *(continued)*

CUT AND INSTALL RISER FORMS.

4

Cut 2× lumber to the correct width and length for your risers. With a circular saw, bevel the outside bottom of each riser, except for the lowest one. Leave about ⅛ inch of each bottom unbeveled for strength. This bevel makes it easier to use trowels to finish the tread after concrete is poured. Install the top riser first and the bottom one last, using at least three double-headed nails or screws.

BRACE THE FORM.

5

Wet concrete is heavy and exerts a great deal of outward pressure on your form. Support the form at all points where it may bulge when the concrete is poured. Make sure none of the braces will get in the way when it comes time to trowel the treads or the landing. For stairs wider than 4 feet, add a riser support by attaching a 2×6 or 2×8 to a 2×4 stake driven deep into the ground near the center of the bottom form. Anchor pointed cleats to the support and to the riser pieces. To shore up the sidewall forms, drive 2×4 stakes into the ground, then nail 1×4 braces to the 2×4s and to the stakes that anchor the sidewall forms. Nail on a 1×4 cross-tie to support the sidewalls.

BUILD FORMS FOR A PARALLEL STAIRWAY.

To build a form for concrete steps that run parallel to the building, strike a level line on the building wall to establish the landing height. Measure from this line to position the plywood forms for the front and side. For deeper stairs, factor in a ¼-inch slope per foot. Brace the plywood pieces with stakes. Cut the beveled riser pieces. Have a helper hold the top and bottom risers level to determine the location of the diagonal brace. Attach it to the house, then attach the risers, cleats, and braces.

BUILDING FORMS FOR WALL FOOTINGS

Footings must be located on undisturbed soil below the frost line. Check your local building codes for requirements regarding size, depth, and metal reinforcement. (See pages 28–29 for how to lay out and excavate for wall footings.) You may not need to build forms; in some situations a trench is enough.

Make footings wide enough to distribute the weight of the wall adequately. Usually this means the footing should be twice as wide as the wall is thick. As a general rule, the thickness of a footing should equal the width of the wall but should not be less than 8 inches.

Install two or three ½-inch reinforcing rods the full length of the footing (see page 41). Also be sure to provide for drainage (see pages 17 and 145). For more information on building forms, see pages 30–31.

CAUTION

STRENGTHEN FORMS BEFORE THE POUR

Weak forms lead to disaster. Once a form bursts or bulges, usually all you can do is let the concrete set, break it into rubble, throw the pieces away, and start over. So always err on the side of caution; overbuild, rather than construct weak concrete forms.

YOU'LL NEED

TIME: About 2 to 3 hours to build 25 feet of forms.

SKILLS: Measuring and cutting, locating corners with a plumb bob, leveling.

TOOLS: Level, hammer, circular saw, small sledgehammer or maul, spade or square shovel.

1

BUILD AND INSTALL FORMS...

The only forming materials you'll need are 2×4s for the footing rails and 1×4s for stakes. Position the stakes (see page 30), then secure the rails to them, making sure the top of each rail is even with or slightly above the top of the stakes.

OR TRENCH AND STAKE.

If the soil is firm enough to hold its shape when filled with wet concrete, dig a trench footing. Keep the sides of the trench even to avoid wasting concrete. For screeding guides, center a row of stakes about 4 feet apart; check the height of the stakes with a line level.

2

SECURE AND LEVEL THE FORMS.

Every few feet along the length of the form, use a carpenter's level to make sure parallel forms are the same height. Also check that the forms are level lengthwise. Drive stakes every 4 feet to anchor the forms securely.

Make sure the stakes penetrate at least 6 inches below the bottom of the footing trench that you will dig (see page 36) to ensure that the form boards will be secure.

Building forms for wall footings *(continued)*

3 DIG THE TRENCH.

Once you are satisfied that the forms are level and secure, excavate an additional 5–6 inches of earth; the total depth of the footing should be no less than 8 inches. Keep the sides of the trench even with the form as you dig. Check the forms again to see that they are level and aligned properly.

STEP DOWN WITH FOOTINGS.

If your site is sloped, you can step down the footings to save concrete. Use 2×8s and additional stakes. For an earth form (lower left), make a wood riser that wedges securely between the two levels. Stepped forms should rise no more than 2 feet per step; the upper and lower forms should overlap by at least 2 feet.

USING PREFAB CONCRETE FORMS

The majority of concrete walls are now formed with reusable, prefabricated forms made of plywood, steel, or aluminum. They can be rented and are available in standard sizes, usually 3, 4, and 8 feet long and a variety of widths. Look under "Concrete Forms" in the business directory of the phone book to find a supplier. The hardware used to install the forms can vary in name; the accessories needed for installation also depend on the type of the forms and the manufacturer . It is important to follow the manufacturer's installation instructions. Don't leave anything to doubt; if you have any questions, consult with the supplier or a concrete professional. Aluminum forms are shown here; general terminology is used to describe the hardware accessories.

YOU'LL NEED

TIME: With help, about one day to build a form for a 4-foot-high, 25-foot-long wall.

SKILLS: General carpentry skills.

TOOLS: Hammer, level, tape measure, metal cutter

INSULATED CONCRETE FORMS

An alternative to building with traditional concrete forms is to use insulated concrete forms. These forms are constructed with insulated foam panels, reinforced with steel rebar to support the concrete pour. They are not removed after the concrete cures, becoming an integral part of the finished wall. Benefits include shielding the home interior from extreme temperatures and external noise, lowering utility bills, and resisting damage from natural disasters. A drawback is that the forms may cost up to 8 percent more than traditional ones.

1 SET FORM AND INSERT CONNECTING PINS.

With a level footing in place, begin to set the forms. While some forms use attached hardware, the system shown here uses a pin and wedge. With at least one wall form set, insert pins into the slots provided.

2 SET WALL TIES.

Once you have an outside and inside form set up, secure the end pieces by placing wall ties on the pins. This locks the inside and outside forms at the specified width of the wall. It also keeps the forms from spreading during the concrete pour. Ties remain in the concrete, becoming a part of the wall.

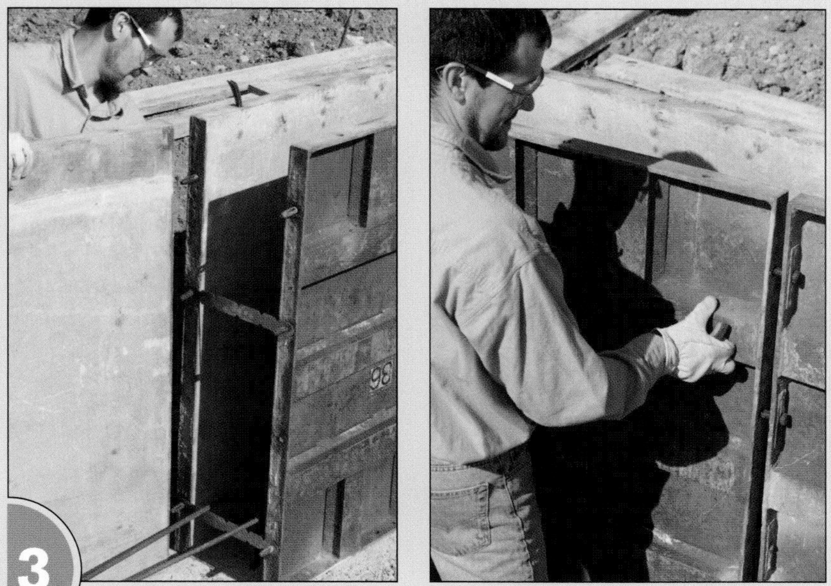

3 CONTINUE TO SET FORMS.

Form set-up can continue in either direction. Continue to set forms by sliding them next to the previously set form and inserting the pin into the slots of the next form.

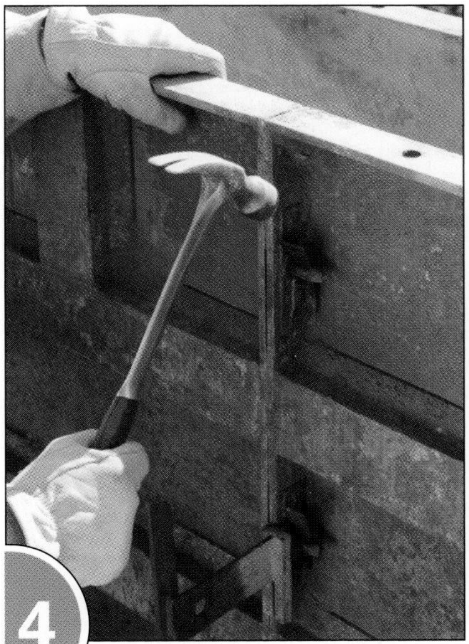

4 SECURE CONNECTING HARDWARE.

Once you have connected two forms together, firmly push the forms together and insert a vertical wedge behind the pin. Tap the wedge with a hammer to secure the connection.

5 CHECK FOR LEVEL AND BRACE.

Make sure all forms are braced to keep them level during the concrete pour and to sustain the weight of the concrete until it achieves the preferred strength. Here one row of waler brackets and 2×6 waler boards were installed at the top of the wall every 8 to 10 feet. An aluminum waler may also be used.

Using prefab concrete forms *(continued)*

TURNING A CORNER

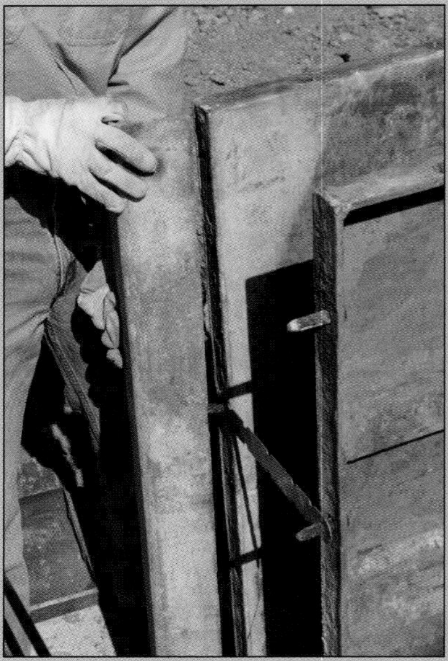

If your project involves a corner, this is a good place to start in setting up your forms. A typical installation will use 90 degree corner forms for inside corners, and outside corners are formed with two standard forms connected by transition brackets. Outside corner forms come in 3-, 4-, 5-, 6-, and 8-foot lengths and are 2 inches wide. There are slots in both sides for the connecting wedge bolt hardware.

Set the corner form and two fillers on a level footing. Connect the fillers to the outside corner form by inserting wedge bolts into the corner form.

TEARDOWN

After the concrete has cured, you can begin to strip the forms. To strip the forms, use a hammer to gently tap loose the pins that were used to secure wall ties, walers, and other hardware. Do not use metal stripping bars on plywood. After the forms have been stripped, portions of the wall ties that were used to keep the forms together during the concrete pour will be left protruding through the sides of the wall. Cut off the protruding pieces.

If properly cared for, prefabricated forms can last through many installations. Most rental stores require that you take responsibility for cleaning and inspecting the forms before you return them. Scrap off any excess concrete left on the forms. Follow any special instructions given by the rental company.

BUILDING COLUMN AND PAD FORMS

Column and pad forms are among the simplest concrete projects. They warrant careful planning, however, because these small pieces of concrete provide essential support for decks, wooden stairways, and outbuildings.

Any outdoor structure that connects to your house should have footings that extend below the frost line. Otherwise, frost heave will stress the junction between the house and the structure and can lead to serious damage. Where frost is not a problem, you usually are safe excavating to a depth of 24 inches.

YOU'LL NEED

TIME: About 1 to 2 hours for most column and pad forms.

SKILLS: No special skills needed.

TOOLS: Posthole digger, round-point shovel, hammer or drill.

INSTALL COLUMN FORMS.

A column form can be nothing more than a hole in the ground. Use a clamshell-type posthole digger or rent a power auger if you have many holes to dig. To save on concrete, try to be precise with your digging. Make the bottom of the hole a bit larger in diameter than the top to "key" it into the ground. Shovel in a few inches of gravel before pouring the concrete. Concrete tube forms save on concrete because they are precisely dimensioned. If you want to continue the column footing above grade, brace the form as shown. Otherwise, shovel in a couple of inches of gravel and set the form in the hole.

MAKE A SMALL CONCRETE PAD.

To make a pad to support heavy items, such as air-conditioners, transformers, or hot tubs, dig out all organic material and build a form of 2×4s. Dig postholes that extend below the frost line to help anchor the pad. Before finishing the pad, check the manufacturer's recommendations regarding the slope required for a particular appliance.

POST-SUPPORT OPTIONS

- Your local building department will have information about the best way to support posts in your area. If you live in a warm area with stable soil, you may be able to skip pouring concrete altogether and instead set a precast concrete pier on a bed of tamped gravel.
- Another effective option is to set a precast pier in a bed of fresh concrete. Twist the pier a little to make sure it bonds firmly to the concrete.
- Avoid post rot by installing a raised post anchor. Some of these you set in concrete; others attach to an embedded bolt.

ADDING REINFORCEMENT

Once the forms are securely in place, double-check them for plumb and level. Prepare the slab area by filling low spots and installing metal reinforcement.

Reinforcement, in the form of 6×6-inch-grid metal mesh or ribbed steel reinforcing rods (rebar), is necessary because concrete is weak under tension. A concrete structure that is larger than a few square feet will crack without such support.

To prevent the forms from absorbing too much water from the concrete and adhering to it, brush sealer on the inside of the forms.

YOU'LL NEED

TIME: About 1 to 2 hours for a medium-size (12×12-foot) slab.

SKILLS: Measuring, cutting.

TOOLS: Shovel, rake, lineman's pliers or hacksaw.

GRADE FOR A SLAB.

Fill in low areas within the forms with gravel or sand, then use a piece of 2×4 to level the area. The 2×4 also acts as a rough depth gauge to show whether you graded deeply enough. Tamp the area firmly, then grade again. If there are gaps between the earth and the bottom of the forms, backfill along the outside edge of the forms with dirt or sand to fill those voids. Otherwise some of the concrete will leak out, wasting material and making it difficult for plants to grow near the edge of the slab.

UNROLL AND PLACE WIRE MESH.

Unroll reinforcing mesh with its curve facing down to help keep it from rolling back into its original shape. Position the wire so its edges reach within 1 to 2 inches of the edge of the finished slab. Place dobies (small concrete blocks) or chairs 2 or 3 feet apart under the mesh so the wire is supported in the vertical center of the slab.

ADD EXPANSION JOINTS.

Whenever new concrete butts up against an existing structure, separate the two with an expansion strip. The gap created allows for expansion of both surfaces and thus prevents cracking. Temporarily hold the expansion strip with bricks or blocks, which you can remove while pouring the concrete. Or nail the strip in place.

FILL IN A STEP FORM.

To save concrete when pouring a deep structure, such as a stairway, fill some of the space with large stones, chunks of broken concrete, or other nonorganic filler material. One way to do this is to lay a low U-shape stone wall about 6 inches from the inside of the sidewall forms and the top riser form. Fill this space with rubble or well-compacted soil. Make sure the concrete will be the correct thickness at every point.

REINFORCE FOOTINGS WITH REBAR.

To strengthen footings, place rebar one-third of the way up from the base of the form. Overlap the rod ends by at least 12 inches and tie them together tightly with wire. This arrangement satisfies most building codes, but check with your local building department to be sure.

For small jobs you can use a hacksaw to cut rebar. Cut it about two-thirds of the way through and bend it until it parts. For large jobs use a circular saw with a carbide-tipped blade.

REINFORCE STEPS.

To prevent steps from cracking or pulling away from the house, attach them solidly to the foundation with rebar. For a concrete foundation, drill holes slightly downward at least 4 inches into the foundation wall. Drive a length of rebar into each hole and bend the rod down to lock it in place. Grout the hole if the rod is not tight. For a hollow concrete block foundation, chisel a hole big enough to stuff paper inside to seal the block's holes at the bottom. Fill the whole cavity with concrete and insert a bent rod. Once the connection to the foundation is made, fashion a grid by tying intersecting rods to those tied to the wall.

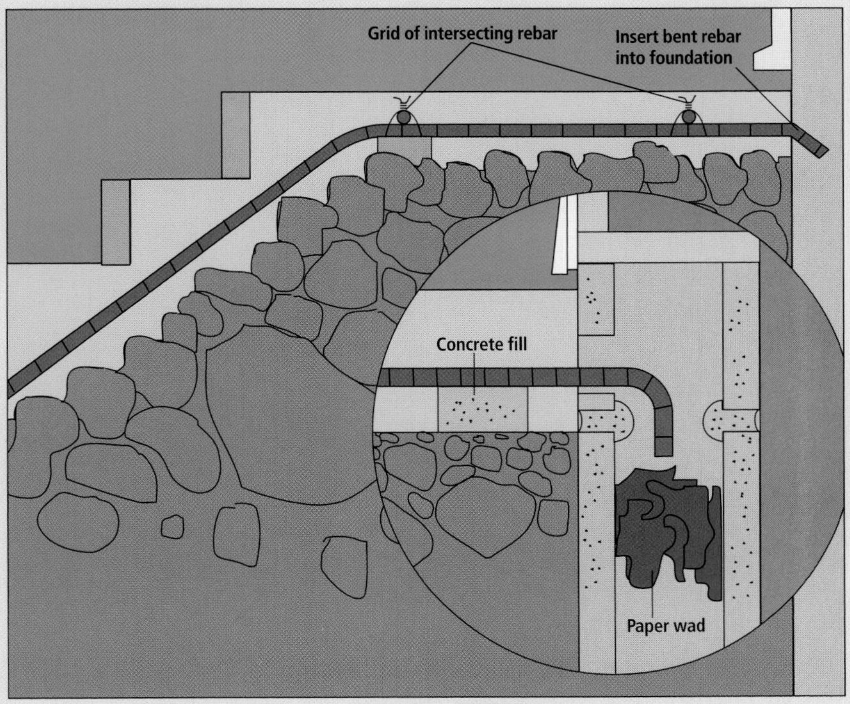

POURING, SCREEDING, AND FLOATING

Once concrete starts to flow, it's too late to alter forms, run for tools, or look for more help. So before you start mixing concrete or before the ready-mix truck arrives, be sure you are ready.

If the compacted base is not still damp from an earlier wetting, sprinkle it and the forms with water to prevent the concrete mix from losing moisture too rapidly. This is especially important on a warm, windy day.

YOU'LL NEED

TIME: About 4 to 8 hours, depending on the slab's size.

SKILLS: Screeding, concrete finishing (a specialized skill that takes a lot of practice to learn).

TOOLS: Shovels, wheelbarrows, rake, screeding straightedge, bull float or darby.

CAUTION

ARE YOU REALLY READY?

- On all but the smallest jobs, have at least two helpers. For a large job, have enough help on hand so some workers can rest occasionally while others keep the wheelbarrows in motion.
- Enlist a bona fide concrete finisher; it's not possible to learn while you try to smooth out the concrete. If you don't have a willing helper who has finished a slab successfully before, hire someone.
- Be sure all reinforcing rods or mesh is in place.
- Have the site inspected the day before the pour, so you will have time to make required changes.

1 MOVE THE CONCRETE ON RAMPS.

Mix your materials as near to the job site as you can. Or have the ready-mix truck park as close as is safe. (Caution: A concrete truck is very heavy and may crack sidewalks or driveways.)

Wet concrete weighs 150 pounds per cubic foot. When wheeling it, keep loads small enough to handle. To cross soft soil or lawns, lay a walkway of 2×10 or 2×12 planks. Build ramps over the forms so you do not disturb them. Use two or more wheelbarrows to keep the job moving; the ready-mix company may charge you for waiting time.

2 DUMP AND MOVE THE CONCRETE.

Start placing fresh material in the farthest corner of the form. Dump it in mounds that reach ½ inch or so above the top of the form. It helps to have one person working a shovel while two or more others run the wheelbarrows. The shoveler directs the wheelbarrow handlers and tells them where to dump the concrete. Wear heavy boots that fit snugly; you will be slogging around in concrete part of the time. Pace your efforts because you'll be moving a considerable amount of concrete before the pour is completed.

3 PULL UP THE REINFORCING MESH.

While pouring the concrete, use a hoe, rake, or shovel to pull the wire mesh up into the concrete. For the greatest strength, keep the mesh positioned halfway between the bottom of the excavation and the finished surface of the slab. Watch that the mesh doesn't get pushed against the form at any point. Keep it 1–2 inches away from all forms.

4 TAMP CONCRETE TO REMOVE AIR POCKETS.

Whether you're pouring a slab, steps, or any other project, take steps to ensure that there are no air pockets, especially at places where a formed edge will be exposed. To do this, run a shovel up and down along the inside edge of all forms and tap the sides of the forms with a hammer. Be sure to check that all corners of the forms are filled in and tamped adequately.

5 SCREED WITH A STRAIGHTEDGE.

Begin screeding (leveling) as soon as you've filled the first 3 or 4 feet of the length of the form. Keep both ends of the screed—a straight 2×4—pressed down on the top of the form while moving it back and forth in a sawing motion and drawing it toward the unleveled concrete. If depressions occur in the screeded surface, throw on a shovel or two of new material, then go back and screed the area again.

6 FLOAT THE SURFACE.

Floating pushes aggregate deeper into the concrete, smooths the surface, and consolidates the wet mixture of fine sand and cement at the top, making further finishing possible. Run a bull float in long, back-and-forth motions, slightly raising its leading edge so it does not dig into the concrete. If you are using a darby, work in large, sweeping arcs. A magnesium float or darby resists sticking better than wood; it should always used for air-entrained concrete.

FINISHING CONCRETE

Finishing concrete is a skill you can't learn quickly. If a project is large or highly visible, have an experienced finisher on hand. If you're a beginner, work on smaller, less prominent projects to develop your new skills.

Timing is critical. If you start too soon, you'll weaken the surface. Start too late and the concrete will be unworkable. The waiting period depends on the weather and type of concrete. Start when the water sheen is gone from the surface and the concrete will carry foot pressure without sinking more than ¼ inch.

YOU'LL NEED

TIME: 1 hour per 50 square feet.

SKILLS: This is a specialized skill learned only with practice.

TOOLS: Steel trowel, edger, groover, plywood for kneelers, circular saw with masonry blade, wooden float, broom.

HIRING A PROFESSIONAL

- If your project is larger than 250 square feet, you may need to hire a professional even if you or a friend have finishing experience. Choose someone who is reliable; if your finisher doesn't show up, you're sunk.
- Check the yellow pages or go to job sites and ask for a finisher. Even if finishers work regularly for a company, many will work for others after-hours. Tell them how many square feet the job is and if there are steps or other complications. They may charge by the area or the hour.

1 EDGE THE CORNERS.

Edging creates rounded edges that prevent damage from chipping and add an attractive finish. Edging also compacts and hardens the concrete along the form. Hold the edger against the form and flat on the concrete surface. Tilt the front edge up slightly while you push it forward; raise the rear slightly when you draw the edger backward. Use short back-and-forth strokes to shape the edge and to work larger pieces of gravel deeper into the concrete. Complete the edging by holding the tool level and using long, smooth strokes. Repeat the edging process after each finishing task.

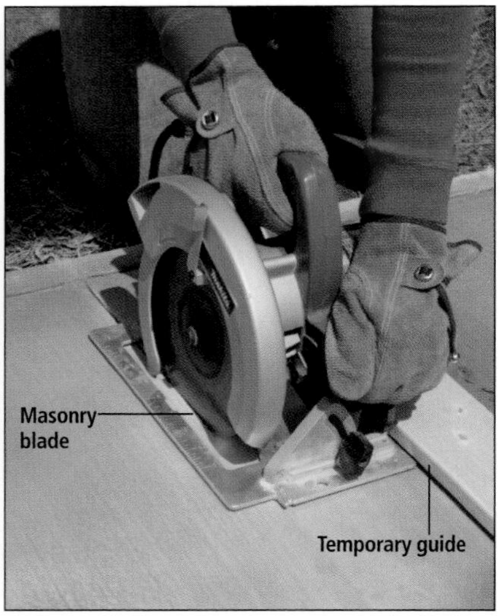

2 MAKE CONTROL JOINTS.

Jointing creates a series of grooves that prevent concrete slabs from cracking randomly. To be effective, a control joint should be one-fourth as deep as the thickness of the slab.

Create control joints in wet concrete with a groover, or saw grooves in the surface after the concrete has hardened. Work the groover as you would an edger, using a straight 2×4 as a guide.

To cut concrete with a circular saw, use a masonry cutting blade. Cut the concrete after the slab is hard, usually 12–24 hours after Step 5. Use a guide to ensure straight cuts.

3

SMOOTH WITH A HAND TOOL.

Smooth the marks left by edging and jointing. Hold a float nearly flat and sweep it in wide arcs. If water surfaces when you begin finishing, stop and wait a while before working again.

4

FINISH WITH A STEEL TROWEL.

To achieve a smooth, dense surface, switch to a steel trowel. Hold the trowel blade nearly flat against the surface, with the leading edge raised slightly. Overlap each pass by one-half of the tool's length so you end up troweling all the surface twice in the first operation. For an even smoother surface, trowel the surface a second or third time. On the final troweling, the trowel should make a ringing sound as you move it over the concrete.

5

MAKE A BROOM FINISH.

For an attractive, slip-resistant surface on steps, walks, and drives, pull a damp broom across just-troweled concrete. The stiffer the bristles, the coarser the texture will be. Only pull the broom—do not push.

Have a brick or a piece of 2×4 handy and occasionally knock the broom against it to keep the bristles clear of concrete buildup.

ADDING CUSTOM FINISHES

Most custom finishes result in a rough-textured surface. But you still need someone with good concrete finishing skills to bring the concrete to the correct level and smoothness to accept the custom finish. One exception is the brick pattern shown on page 47. For that project, most do-it-yourselfers can start with a tamped sand or gravel bed, mix and pour small amounts of concrete at a time, and proceed from one form to the next.

YOU'LL NEED

TIME: About 1 to 2 additional hours of work for a medium-size (12×12-foot) slab. Limit the size of the job so the concrete will not set up before you finish.

SKILLS: Concrete finishing.

TOOLS: Garden hose, trowels, brushes, joint strike.

FINISHING OPTIONS

- For a broom finish, trowel the concrete as described on page 45. Then use a straw broom to make swirling patterns on the surface, using wide arcs or squiggly strokes.
- You can rent concrete embossing stampers in many patterns. They work best if your concrete contains gravel no larger than ¼ inch. To move the job along, rent at least two stampers. When the surface has begun to set but is still soft, press the stamper in place firmly by stepping on it. Work quickly, alternating stampers.

Making an aggregate surface

1 SPRINKLE STONES ON THE SURFACE.

Pour the concrete and screed it to the top of the forms. As soon as the water evaporates from the surface (watch carefully), sprinkle stones in a uniform layer over the concrete.

2 PUSH THE STONES IN.

With a wooden float, carefully press the stones into the concrete until the surface is smooth, even, and as free of stroke marks as a floated slab. If the slab is large, apply a curing retarder to give you extra working time.

3 EXPOSE THE STONES.

When the concrete becomes firm (after about an hour), gently brush away excess concrete with a stiff broom. If the stones come out, stop working and wait for the concrete to harden further. Spray a fine mist on the surface. Continue sweeping until runoff water is clear and the stones are exposed.

MAKE A TRAVERTINE FINISH.

This finish should be used only in areas not subject to freezing. Pour, screed, and float the concrete. As soon as the water evaporates from the surface, use a brush to spatter on pigmented mortar the consistency of thick paint. After the mortar has stiffened slightly, use a steel trowel to smooth the high spots to make the distinctive travertine pattern.

ROCK-SALT FINISH

This technique produces fairly deep pits in the concrete surface, giving it a weathered appearance. Like the travertine finish, left, it is not recommended for areas subject to freezing. Water sits in the pits and freezes, cracking the surface of the concrete.

After finishing the concrete, sprinkle some rock salt—not too much or you'll weaken the slab—over the surface. Use a trowel to embed the salt in the concrete. After the concrete hardens, wash and brush away the remaining salt.

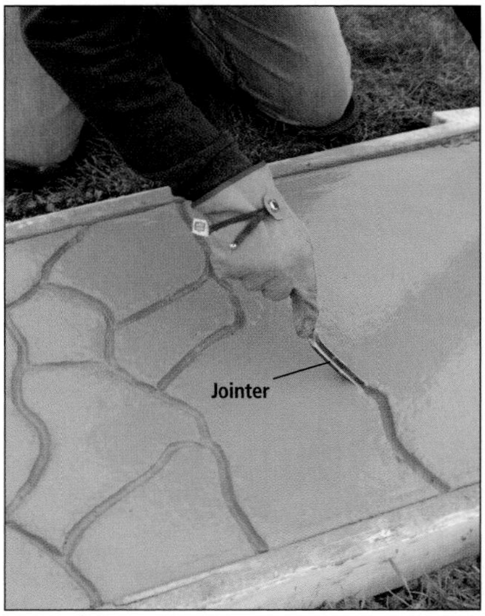

CARVE A FLAGSTONE PATTERN.

To make your surface look like flagstones or geometric shapes, score the concrete soon after you finish it and after water has evaporated from the surface. A concave jointer works well for this technique. Go over the marks each time you do other finishing operations.

Making a brick pattern

1 POUR CONCRETE INTO A FORM.

Ideal for small jobs, these brick-shape forms are available at home centers. Set a form on top of the gravel or sand bed and shovel concrete into it. Make sure each section is filled to the top of the form but no higher.

2 REMOVE THE FORM AND FINISH WITH A TROWEL.

After water has evaporated from the concrete surface, wiggle the form out carefully so clean-looking lines remain. Flick away crumbs and carefully give the surface a trowel finish. Once the concrete is cured, fill the gaps with mortar.

ADDING COLOR TO CONCRETE

White and various shades of tan concrete can be ordered ready-made from some suppliers; they simply adjust the mix of raw materials to achieve the color. For more intense colors, you can add pigment to the concrete as it is mixed. This makes sense only if you need color throughout the slab, as you might for a rough broom finish or aggregate surfaces, or on steps, walkway, or patios where the edges of the slab show. If you mix several batches of concrete, it's difficult to keep the color consistent. Most often you'll need or want to add pigment only to the surface, where the color shows.

YOU'LL NEED

TIME: About 2 hours per 100 square feet of concrete.

SKILLS: Careful spreading of the pigment powder.

TOOLS: Concrete finishing tools.

PAINT OR STAIN.

The safest coloring method is to wait for the concrete to cure and then apply special concrete stain or paint.

Chemical stains yield better results than paint. Stains are applied when the concrete is cured completely and are designed to seep into the concrete and bond with it, producing a color that lasts longer than paint.

Paint adheres to the surface only. Some are durable, but with heavy use even the best paints wear away and require another coat every few years.

APPLY PIGMENT-CURING COMPOUND.

Curing pigmented concrete is tricky. The normal curing techniques (see page 49) are not recommended because they can cause the color to become uneven. Check the pigment manufacturer's recommendations, which often involve spraying the concrete with a special curing compound designed for colored concrete. Mix this compound and spray it on. After curing and drying, seal the surface with a nonwax, polymeric sealer to accentuate the color and make cleaning easy.

CURING CONCRETE

Proper curing can make or break a concrete project. Hydration, the chemical process that hardens cement, stops after the concrete first sets unless you keep it moist and fairly warm. Without adequate hydration, the concrete will be weak.

Whether you choose to cover or periodically spray the concrete, keep it damp or wet for several days after pouring it. If the weather is cold, insulate the concrete during curing by spreading straw over the top of it.

YOU'LL NEED

TIME: Periodic attention over several days.

SKILLS: No special skills needed.

TOOLS: Garden hose, sprinkler.

COVER WITH BURLAP OR PLASTIC.

The most effective curing method is to cover the concrete surface with burlap or old blankets and keep them wet with frequent waterings. Be sure the fabric is clean so you won't stain the concrete. Place the covering on the concrete as soon as it is hard enough to resist surface damage. Weigh down the covering with scraps of lumber.

If you cannot wet the surface periodically, cover it with plastic sheeting. This traps moisture and works as well as wet cloth.

KEEP A SPRINKLER RUNNING.

Frequent wetting with a lawn sprinkler, especially during daylight hours in the summer, also provides the moisture concrete needs to cure slowly. Before spraying the water, make sure the concrete is set hard enough so the spray will not damage the surface. If you apply too much water before the concrete is set, it could cause spalling or chipping at a later date. Avoid cycles of wetting and drying.

COVER WITH STRAW IF IT GETS COLD.

If cold weather strikes after the pour, spread 6–12 inches of dry straw or hay over the concrete, then cover the straw with canvas or plastic sheeting. Be especially careful to cover the edges and corners of slabs, the places most likely to freeze.

Laying PATIOS AND WALKS

Patios expand living space into the outdoors. They can function as outdoor rooms for almost any activity–cooking, entertaining, or relaxing.

Laying a path or walkway establishes a journey. Whether the destination is defined with an entry or transition of space, the journey itself becomes the focus when you create a charming, well-constructed path or walkway. Selecting the right material for the walk can define the journey. The use of masonry–be it bricks or pavers–can create a path that will make the journey enjoyable.

Begin your patio or walkway project with a few inspirational ideas, found on pages 52–55. Once you've envisioned your own dream project, see pages 56–75 to learn how to plan and install it yourself.

PLAYFUL PATH
This parquet walkway was created using pavers and pebbles. Edging keeps the pebbles where they belong. See page 71 for information about installing loose materials.

FUNCTIONAL OASIS
Integrating a brick patio into the design of this serene garden oasis provides a grounding element for the space and adds both interest and functionality. The gazebo offers a spot for relaxation. The addition of a table and chairs creates a setting for dining and entertaining.

WELCOMING WALKWAY
Kiln-fired pavers allow you to roll out the red carpet for friends and guests. Pattern variations make it easy to apply a signature look. The kiln-firing creates a durable, long-lasting surface that will bear the brunt of seasonal extremes.

SAND AND STONE
A sand bed serves as a base for this stone walkway. The stones are fitted by hand in a way that minimizes the gaps between them. Set the stones by pouring a concrete sand mix over them and sweeping away the excess. Complete the look by cleaning the surface with a mist of water. The final effect is a walkway that appears to have been laboriously set by hand in concrete.

FORMAL AFFAIR
Brick fosters a formal feel for this courtyard. The exposed-aggregate concrete adds a natural touch. Together they make a bold first impression.

GREATNESS OF GRAVEL
This gravel patio is inexpensive and easy to build, and if installed properly, requires very little maintenance. The crunchy sound makes walking upon it a pleasure.

>

GRACEFUL CURVE
Rather than plotting the shortest distance between two points, a curved path traverses the distance with grace.

<

WELCOME TO YOUR RETREAT
Large, flat stones fit together like a puzzle to form a meandering path and garden-enclosed patio area in this restful landscape. This chapter provides all the step-by-step techniques you'll need to create your own backyard getaway.

MEDITERRANEAN STYLE
Muted red brick in a basket-weave pattern is the perfect match for this Mediterranean-style courtyard. Setting the bricks in sand without mortar (see pages 62–65) gives the patio its Spanish feel.

PATIO PUZZLE
Large slabs of Colorado red sandstone form this remote retreat tucked in the corner of a backyard. Placing these large pieces is similar to solving a large puzzle except this puzzle requires an abundance of muscle and patience (see pages 66–67).

GARDEN-SIDE RETREAT
Interlocking brick pavers provide visual interest and texture and give this patio a feeling of comfort that embraces guests.

RUSTIC CHARM
Terra-cotta tiles furnish this courtyard patio with informality. The reddish tiles are the perfect choice for a Spanish Colonial-style home. However, the softness of terra-cotta makes it a high-maintenance material.

PLANNING PATIOS AND WALKWAYS

For patios or walkways, choose patterns and materials that complement your yard. Avoid a boring patio made out of only one material, but don't go overboard by mixing in too many disparate elements. A theme with variations works best: Choose one or two materials or patterns that please you and repeat them in different locations. For example, use the same type of timbers for the patio edging and for a raised planter nearby.

Plan the space

Stand on the site with your family and envision your future patio. Discuss how each person intends to use the space. Set your lawn furniture, barbecue grill, toys, and other items in the places where they will be used. Mark out an ideal layout, using a rope or length of garden hose. Make sure there will be enough room for traffic as well as comfortable seating.

Once you have an idea you are comfortable with, make a sketch. It doesn't have to be perfect. At this point you are more interested in the general layout, traffic patterns, and views than in the details.

Put it on paper

To help with your planning, try to locate the plat, a scaled map that shows the size and shape of your property. It will also show any easements adjacent to your land. If you don't have a copy of your plat, check with your city or county zoning or assessor's office. They may have one on file and be able to provide you with a copy for minimal cost. Make several copies of the plat.

Transfer the plat or measure out and record the dimensions of your property onto a sheet of graph paper. Indicate which direction is north so anyone who picks up the diagram will be able to read it properly. Next indicate the position and outline of major structures on your property, such as the house, garage, and shed. Then sketch in landscape features—it will be helpful later to indicate the trees and foliage with lightly shaded patterns. Once you complete the drawing to your satisfaction, make copies so you can draw out different ideas for patio and walkway shapes based on your initial sketches.

Harmonize with your home

Maintaining visual harmony with the existing house and structures is important. Consider materials and scale. The patio or walkway should be compatible with the surrounding elements, neither overwhelming them nor being overpowered by them. The best ideas incorporate key features from existing structures, hardscapes, and plantings. You don't need to reproduce these elements precisely; structural materials and accents should be selected to blend with the overall property.

Think about transitions

It's natural to get caught up in the excitement of the new outdoor area you are creating. But don't forget to consider the transition from inside to outside. You may find it necessary to relocate or install a door or window to connect an indoor room to your new outdoor room. If so, think through

how a new doorway will impact existing interior rooms. If you plan to use your patio as an outdoor kitchen, for example, it would be helpful to be able to access it from your indoor kitchen to ease the preparation and serving of food. Try to key in on elements that can ease the transition from one space to another, such as an accent color or theme.

Set a budget

Budgets allow you to evaluate all the things you imagine and to prioritize them so you can achieve your goal. Set a limit on what you will spend for the project. List everything you believe is a necessity. Make a separate wish list of accessories. Keep the two lists separate until you have finalized the costs of the "necessities" list. Add a 10-percent buffer for cost overruns and unexpected changes to the plans, such as removing an old septic tank you didn't realize was buried in the backyard.

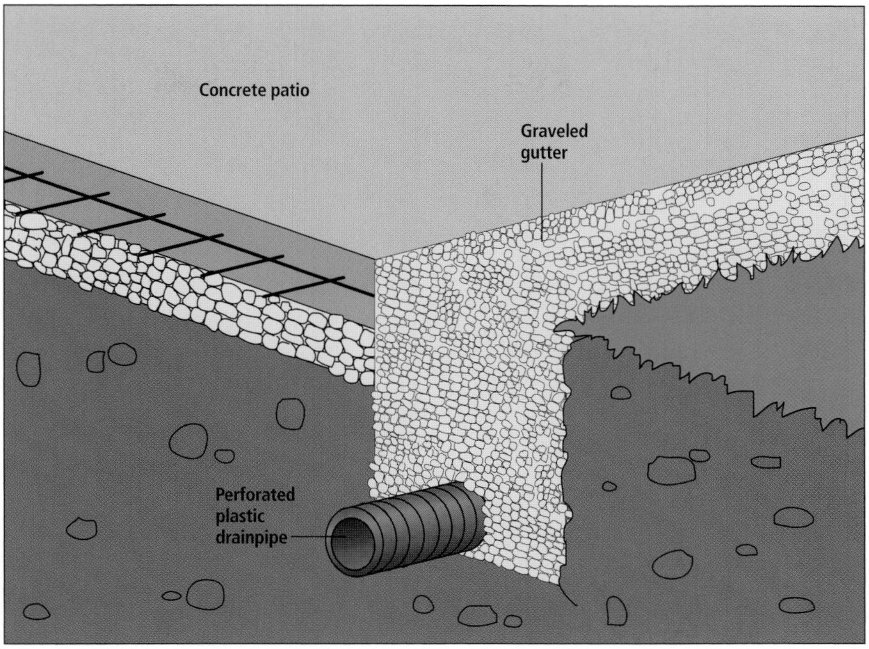

PLAN ADEQUATE DRAINAGE.

A patio made of bricks set in sand allows only a small amount of water to seep through. A slab or a patio of mortared brick or stone will shed all water. In most cases a mulched flower bed or a gravel- or loose-fill trench around the perimeter of the patio or path will provide sufficient drainage. Always make sure the surface is sloped away from the house. (To cope with more serious drainage problems, see page 24.)

LANDSCAPE CONSIDERATIONS
A large, established tree didn't undermine plans for this backyard patio. An innovative design and careful choice of materials will allow the tree to continue to flourish. The low stone wall serves double duty as additional seating. Because the flagstone is set in a sand bed, moisture can reach the tree roots. A landscape fabric beneath the sand inhibits the growth of weeds.

Planning patios and walkways *(continued)*

CREATING INTEREST
When using only one material for a patio, you need not be limited to a uniform surface. Insets of finished concrete set off the washed aggregate surface of this open patio. A stone path leads from the dining area to a more remote patio with a lush garden backdrop.

EASY ACCESS
French doors conveniently connect this patio to the house. The classic red brick elevates the strong vertical and horizontal lines of this formal entertaining area and echoes the color of the warm redwood trellis.

GO NATURAL
Use of native materials enables a patio to blend into its environment. Here native flagstone set in concrete produces an attractive, agrarian patio that wanders through the garden area.

GARDEN WELCOME
A flagstone pathway extends an invitation to wander along this garden path (see pages 66–67). The natural beauty of the stone works well with the stacked rock wall (see page 82–83).

CHOOSING A PATTERN

Many brick patterns have been developed over the years by installers. The modular shape of bricks lends itself to forming interesting designs. The layout is usually fairly simple. Some patterns, such as a pinwheel, do require planning and thought. Curved and irregular-shape bricks and pavers can be purchased at an added cost.

Choose a pattern

The patio patterns shown below work well for bricks or pavers that are twice as long as they are wide. The diagonal herringbone pattern requires you to cut a large number of bricks at a 45-degree angle. Try using one pattern for a border and another for the main surface.

BRICK AND PAVER PATTERNS

Diagonal herringbone

Double basket weave

Basket weave

Running bond

Straight bond

Half-square

Stagger step

Pinwheel

Straight herringbone

SELECTING EDGING MATERIALS

Edging materials usually are sunk lower into the ground than the rest of the patio to provide a stable framework. For the best border appearance, use the same material as the patio surface or choose a material that creates a pleasant contrast between the patio and yard. If your patio is made of loose material, such as crushed stone, be sure the edging seals it in and is high enough to keep stones from scattering into the grass. If grass comes right up to the patio, choose an edging that is lawn-mower-friendly, such as a smooth, raised edge.

YOU'LL NEED

TIME: About 1 to 3 hours per 10 feet of edging.

SKILLS: Leveling materials.

TOOLS: Depending on the edging: shovel, trowel, rake, tamper, small sledgehammer, brick set.

KEEP YOUR CLIMATE IN MIND

If you live in an area subject to frost, your patio will "float"—rise and fall 1 to 2 inches—from winter to spring. It does not make sense to install a concrete edging that extends below the frost line, but you do want something substantial that firmly holds the patio materials in place. Plastic edging, upright timbers, tilted brick soldiers, and upright soldiers are less secure than concrete, heavy timbers, and edgings that are staked strongly.

Concrete: Formed concrete edging is the best retainer of patio materials. Dig a 6-inch-deep trench, tamp, add 2–3 inches of gravel, build forms, and pour concrete.

Upright (soldier) bricks or pavers: Edging or pavers should rest on a concrete footing. Set them in concrete when it's wet or set them in mortar after the concrete cures.

Tilted soldiers: To install a tilted edging of bricks or pavers, dig a trench 8 inches deep, tamp, add 2–3 inches of sand, and set the bricks. Backfill and tamp firmly.

Flagstone edging: Flagstones can be set in well-tamped ground. Make adjustments as you go, digging or adding soil to keep the top edges of the stones fairly even.

Landscaping timbers or railroad ties: This strong edging is quick to construct. Dig a trench, tamp, and add 2 inches of sand. Place the timber, drill holes, and drive in spikes or rebar.

Upright half-round logs: Cut the logs with a chainsaw; 16- to 24-inch lengths work well. Treat the bottoms to prevent rot. Dig a trench, add gravel and sand, and install logs.

Lumber: Choose pressure-treated lumber or heartwood of redwood or cedar. Set 2×4s in a shallow trench and support them with metal stakes.

Steel ribbon: This works well for curves. Mark a curved line on the ground and tap the metal into the ground. Pound in retaining stakes through premade slots in the edging.

Plastic edging: Plastic is cheap and easy, but seldom holds its shape and may crack. Slice a line in the ground with a shovel and push the edging into it. Reinforce with stakes.

LAYING BRICK PATIOS IN SAND

Set bricks or other paving materials in a well-tamped bed of sand, and you'll have a flexible but firm patio surface that will stand up to years of use, even in areas subject to frost. A brick-in-sand patio is an ideal do-it-yourself project. But carrying the bricks and digging, smoothing, and tamping the patio surface involves hard work that will put a strain on your back. Don't tackle everything by yourself; have helpers on hand.

YOU'LL NEED

TIME: Several days to dig and lay an 80-square-foot patio.

SKILLS: Measuring, leveling, laying out square lines, cutting bricks, setting bricks.

TOOLS: Round-point shovel, spade, line or water level, hose, carpenter's level, hammer, brick set, small sledgehammer, screed, circular saw with masonry blade, broom, rubber mallet.

HOW MUCH BEDDING?

Adequate bedding is essential for a patio to remain smooth and level for years to come. If you live in an area with periods of heavy rain or winters with below-freezing temperatures, a brick-in-sand patio should rest on a bed of 1 to 2 inches of tamped sand that, in turn, rests on 4 to 6 inches of tamped gravel. In dry climates with soils that have a heavy clay, sand, or rock content, a sand base alone may be sufficient. Check with your building department to see what is required in your area.

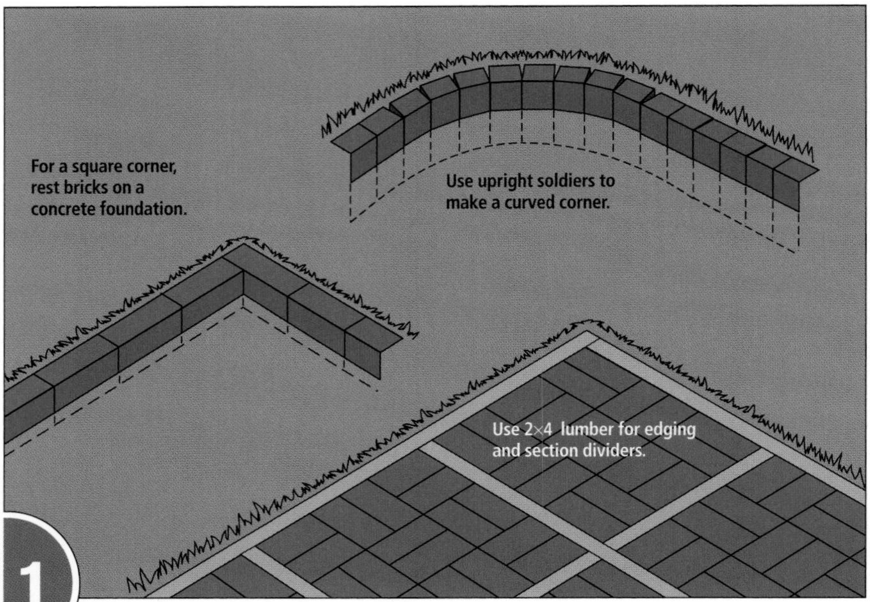

1 LAY OUT THE SITE.

Use the techniques on pages 24–25 to lay out the site. Use the 3-4-5 method to establish square corners and use a line level or water level to establish the correct slope, about ¼ inch per running foot. If your yard already slopes a bit, but not more than ½ inch per foot, you can follow its contour so you will not have to fill in and resod the lawn after building the patio. Select the style of edging and the brick pattern you want.

2 EXCAVATE AND TAMP.

Remove the sod and dig to the correct depth, removing roots 1 inch or larger in diameter. The paving material should be 1 inch above grade. Dig out the soil for the edging and patio to a depth that leaves room for adequate bedding material. Adjust the surface height by using more or less bedding material. Tamp the ground firmly, especially if you have not reached undisturbed claylike soil.

3 INSTALL THE EDGING.

Stretch a mason's line to serve as a guide for the height and alignment of the edging. For the brick soldiers shown here, place a small amount of sand in the bottom of the excavation and tap the bricks with the handle of your trowel to set them at the height you want. Fill around the sides of each brick with sand as you work. Backfill with just enough soil to keep the bricks from leaning outward. For other edging options, see page 61.

PREPARING THE GROUND WITH A TAMPER

It is important that the ground under the sand-and-gravel bed be firm. In most cases, that means tamping each layer. For small areas you can use a piece of 4×4 or a fence post for tamping. Or make a tamper from plywood and 2× lumber like the one shown on page 125. Small hand tampers can be rented also.

For large patios consider renting a vibrating power tamper. Transporting it to the work site requires some heavy lifting, but once you get it there, it speeds up the tamping process dramatically.

4 COVER WITH LANDSCAPING FABRIC.

If your bedding is only sand, cover the tamped soil with landscaping fabric before adding the sand. The fabric reduces weed growth but allows water to filter through into the soil. For a sand-and-gravel bed, lay the fabric on top of the tamped gravel. Overlap the sheets about 2 inches.

Laying brick patios in sand *(continued)*

5

SCREED THE SAND.

Shovel in the sand to roughly the correct height. Dampen it and tamp it down. Draw a straightedge across the sand to smooth it out. For this purpose make a screed out of a straight 2×4 with a length of 1×4 or 1×6 nailed to it. If the patio is wider than 8 feet, you will need to install temporary supports for screeding. With a helper, work the screed back and forth as you move it sideways to achieve a level surface.

CROWN A WALK.

When screeding a walkway, give it a slight crown so water will run off easily. Make a screed with a curved cut, as shown. Pull it across the edging or forms as you would with a flat screed.

6

LAY THE BRICKS.

Starting in a corner, begin laying the bricks or pavers. Set them straight down rather than sliding them into place so as not to disturb the level sand surface. Place each brick snugly against its neighbors and tap it gently with a rubber mallet or block of wood. Use a level to check for proper slope and to make sure the bricks are all at the same height.

If a brick is too low, pick it up, trowel in more sand, and tap it into place until it rests at the correct height.

7

CHECK FOR STRAIGHTNESS.

Every third or fourth course, use a taut string line as a guide to make sure you are laying the bricks in straight lines and at the proper elevation. Do not step or kneel on the bricks as you work; use a piece of plywood as a kneeler.

8 CUT BRICKS TO FIT.

To cut a brick or paver by hand, score it all the way around by tapping a brick set with a small sledgehammer. Place the brick on a bed of sand or loose soil and give it a sharp blow with a brick set.

For a cleaner-looking cut, use a circular saw with a masonry cutting blade. With either method be sure to wear gloves and eye and ear protection.

CAUTION

FOR LARGE JOBS, USE A MASONRY CUTOFF SAW

If you have many bricks to cut, a circular saw may not be up to the job. Cutting will be slow, and you'll have to change blades frequently. Worst of all, the brick dust and general wear and tear may burn out your saw.
Rent a masonry cutoff saw instead. This is a large power saw equipped with a long-lasting blade. With it you can cut crisp lines with ease all day long, which speeds up the job significantly. Or rent a wet-cutting masonry/brick saw.

9 FILL THE JOINTS.

When all the bricks or pavers are in place, spread a thin layer of fine sand over the patio surface and gently sweep back and forth so the sand fills the joints. Be especially careful at first so you don't dislodge the bricks. Once the joints are full of sand, hose off the entire surface with a fine spray to wash away the remaining sand particles. This compacts the sand and forces it into the joints. Repeat this process, sweeping in more sand and spraying until the sand is level with the top of the bricks.

FILLING JOINTS WITH THE DRY MORTAR METHOD

You can make your patio more permanent by using dry mortar mix rather than plain sand in the joints. For this method leave ½-inch spaces between the bricks when you set them in place. Sweep the dry mortar mix into the joints, remove excess mortar, and sprinkle the surface gently with water until the mix is wet. Repeat the sprinkling process twice at 15-minute intervals to ensure you have enough water in the mortar. The mortar will harden within a few hours and cure in a week. This method is not recommended if the soil in your area freezes; the mortar lines will crack.

LAYING FLAGSTONE SURFACES

The simplest method of installing a flagstone patio is to place the stones on well-tamped soil. Such a patio surface is quick to install; however, you'll need to readjust settled stones every year.

The flagstones should be at least ¾ inch thick or they will crack. Purchase stones of a fairly uniform thickness so they will be easy to lay evenly. If you choose a combination of large, medium, and small stones, you'll be able to make creative patterns more easily.

YOU'LL NEED

TIME: 1 day to excavate and lay a 100-square-foot patio.

SKILLS: Excavating, cutting, and laying stones.

TOOLS: Shovel, tamper, rake, brick set, small sledgehammer, hose.

OTHER METHODS OF LAYING FLAGSTONE

You can lay flagstones in a sand bed, as you would bricks or pavers (see pages 62–65), by filling the joints with sand or soil, tamping it in gently, and allowing grass or moss to grow in the joints.

Or you can cover a concrete slab with flagstone, laying it in mortar as you would stone or tile veneer (see pages 72–75). If you use this method, be sure to dry-lay the stones before mixing the mortar so you can set them in place quickly. Otherwise you'll have a mess on your hands as you try various stones to see if they fit.

1 LAY OUT THE PERIMETER.

Flagstone patios look best if they don't have sharp edges. One way to create graceful curves is with a water hose. Charge the hose by closing the nozzle and turning on the water; this helps the hose hold its shape. Lay out the hose in the shape you choose and pour flour or sand all along its length. When you remove the hose, you'll have a clear line marking the excavation area.

2 EXCAVATE AND TAMP.

Dig up the sod. Remove all significant organic material, including tree roots ½ inch thick or larger. If you don't, the patio will settle unevenly as the roots rot. You may have to dig deeper than the thickness of the stones; if so, fill in any low spots with sand or soil, then tamp firm. Rake the area level and tamp the soil firmly with a hand tamper (use a power vibrating tamper for larger areas). Fill in and retamp low spots. Install edging, if desired, before you lay the stones.

3 LAY THE STONES.

Start with large stones around the perimeter. If a stone is too high, pick it up and dig out some soil; if it's too low, add some soil or sand beneath it. Test each stone to make sure it does not rock. Work slowly and take breaks; this kind of labor can harm your back even if you do not feel a strain.

4 CUT STONES WHERE NECESSARY.

Wherever possible use uncut stones. When you have to cut a stone, lay it over the stone it will adjoin and trace the outline with chalk, a pencil, or a scratching tool.

Use a brick set and small sledgehammer to score the line, making a groove about ⅛ inch deep. Set the stone on top of a scrap piece of wood. For large stones have someone stand on the other end (as shown above). Split the stone with a single blow from the sledgehammer. If the scrap piece is large enough to use elsewhere, protect it with a lumber scrap. You may have to make more than one split if you need a curved edge on a stone.

PLEASING PATTERNS

- The trick to a professional-looking flagstone surface is keeping the gaps between stones consistent. Test your gaps with a scrap piece of wood; a piece of ½-inch plywood works well.
- Mix the sizes of the flagstones evenly. Make separate piles of small, medium, and large stones. Select from the piles alternately so you won't end up with a lot of small stones in one corner of the patio and big stones in another.
- Keep trying; there's no shortcut to making a pleasing pattern. You'll have to test different configurations and occasionally cut a stone to maintain good-looking gaps.

5 FILL THE JOINTS.

Shovel dirt into the gaps between the stones, taking care not to get too much on the stones. Wet the patio surface with a fine spray, cleaning the stones while thoroughly wetting the soil. Fill in low spots, spray again, and repeat until you have level-looking joints that are about ⅛ inch below the surface of the stones. Plant the gaps with grass seed, moss, or a low-growing groundcover to discourage weeds from growing.

LAYING PAVER PATIOS

Concrete pavers come in a variety of shapes, sizes, and colors. Stronger and denser than ordinary concrete blocks, they resist moisture absorption and damage from repeated freeze-thaw cycles. New styles of pavers interlock in a variety of geometric patterns. Your design can be casual or formal.

Take measurements with you when you're ready to purchase pavers. Most retailers will assist you with estimating the number of pavers, amount of gravel, and volume of sand you will need. Buy extra pavers to compensate for breakage and incorrect cuts, and to keep on hand for future repairs.

Before you begin any work, have the local utility company or locating service check for underground pipes and wires. They will mark the location and depth of utilities.

YOU'LL NEED

TIME: One day to excavate and lay a 100-square-foot patio.

SKILLS: Measuring, leveling, laying out square lines, cutting pavers, setting pavers.

TOOLS: Round-point shovel, spade, line or water level, hose, carpenter's level, hammer, brick set, small sledgehammer, screed, masonry chisel, rubber mallet, circular saw with masonry blade, broom.

THE PROPER DEPTH

Soil conditions vary greatly. Excavating to the proper depth is important, especially if your region experiences freezing temperatures and frost heave. Contact your local area extension office or building inspector for guidance.

1 EXCAVATE THE SITE.

Mark the perimeter of the patio by either driving stakes into the ground or using a garden hose and flour to mark curves (see pages 24–26). Remove the sod and soil. Dig down 4–8 inches for a gravel or crushed stone base, plus 2 inches for a sand bed, plus the thickness of the pavers. Slide a 2×4 along the surface to create a fairly level plane for the base.

2 SET THE BASE.

Check the condition of the excavated area. If soil is loose, rent a tamper for clay soil or a vibrating plate for sandy soil. Lay the crushed stone base, spreading it evenly, and compact it. For best compaction place the base material in "lifts" no more than 4 inches in depth at a time. A crushed rock base with an abundance of fine particles will compact firmly and create a solid base.

3 INSTALL GROUND FABRIC.

Cover the base with a layer of ground fabric. It will act as a filter to prevent erosion occurring from drainage through the pavers and will inhibit weeds with deep taproots from finding their way to the surface.

4 FASTEN THE EDGING.

The border or edge restraints keep the edge blocks from drifting and creating gaps. Various edging options are available; plastic trim is the most popular. Lay out the trim and use a small sledgehammer to drive oversize stakes to secure it in place.

5 ADD SAND FOR THE SETTING BED.

Shovel sand over the base. No more than 1–2 inches is necessary. Concrete sand, coarse-washed concrete sand, or granite stone dust make the best setting beds. Use a 2×4 or 2×6, notched so the bottom is at the top height for the setting bed, as a screed board to level the sand bed (see page 64).

6 LAY THE PAVERS.

Lay the pavers using a 4-foot carpenter's level to check the surface as you complete a section. Fill low spots. Tap raised pavers using a rubber mallet. Pavers vary in size and shape, so there is no single starting point or method for placing them. To maintain a uniform color mix, use pavers from the same bundle or pallet; to create interest, mix colors.

7 CUT PAVERS TO FIT.

No matter what the shape of the pavers, you may end up with voids along the edges. Sometimes you can buy edging pieces to fill those spaces. Otherwise you'll have to cut pavers to fit. You can break pavers using a masonry chisel and hammer or make precise cuts using a circular saw with a masonry blade.

8 FINISH WITH SAND.

Spread clean sand on the surface and sweep it thoroughly into the joints–this helps hold the pavers in place. Spray fine mist over the surface using a garden hose to settle the sand. Repeat two to three times or until the gaps are filled. Some types of pavers require sealing—check with your supplier. Sealing also accentuates the pavers' color while protecting them from staining. Sealing does require periodic reapplication.

PLAN YOUR PROJECT FOR THE PERFECT FINISH

The space you need. Patios and walkways should be wide enough to comfortably accommodate people and furniture. Paths and walkways should be at least 3 feet wide; a wider path creates an atmosphere of elegance and grace.

Sweeping accents. People enjoy wandering along paths with gentle, sweeping curves. Pavers can accent and expand planting beds.

Environment. Be sure to take into account water drainage. Slope all surfaces away from the house.

Extending the day. Outdoor lighting defines your patio and walkway while providing safety and expanding usage into the evening. You can light up the area from above using spotlights or accent the space with low-voltage fixtures.

LAYING STEPPING-STONES

A stepping-stone path is among the easiest improvements you can make to your yard. Consider it for out-of-the-way areas where you won't need to wheel a cart or a stroller. Stepping-stones also make an ideal path through decorative groundcover; they'll almost blend into the foliage.

When laying stones on a lawn, make sure your mower has enough clearance to go over the stones without damaging the blade.

YOU'LL NEED

TIME: About 1–2 hours to lay a path with 10 stones.

SKILLS: No special skills needed.

TOOLS: Round-point shovel, garden trowel.

SELECTING STEPPING-STONES

At a building center or patio supply center, you'll find a variety of stepping-stone materials. Popular manufactured materials include cast concrete circles with exposed aggregate (as shown at right), as well as octagonal or square concrete pavers.

For a more natural look, you can select large, round flagstones. Large river rocks also work, but be sure they have a fairly flat surface or mowing over them will be difficult. Although they won't last as long as concrete or stone, cross sections of logs, 1 foot in diameter or larger, make an attractive path.

CUT IN AND LEVEL THE STEPPING-STONES.

Arrange the stones on your lawn and let several short and tall people try them out to make sure the pattern allows for easy, natural walking. Once you've got the stones where you want them, mark each stone's position by slicing into the turf around its perimeter with a shovel or spade. Remove the stone and dig out the sod and organic material. Tamp down the soil, fill in low spots, and retamp. Be sure that the top of each stone is only about ¼ inch above ground level so you can safely run a lawn mower over the stones. Place the stone in the hole and test for height and stability. Make sure the stone doesn't rock as it is stepped on. Add or dig out soil if necessary to level the stone.

Stepping-stones sink over time. Plan on prying them out and reseating them every few years.

INSTALLING LOOSE PAVING MATERIALS

Walkways made of loose paving materials are easy to install and comfortable to walk on. Pressure-treated 4×4s make an attractive permanent edging, but you also can use brick soldiers, metal or plastic edging, or concrete. One drawback to this type of walkway is that some loose material, such as pea gravel or river rock, is kicked up easily and makes mowing difficult. Also loose material can compact or degrade over time and may need to be replenished.

YOU'LL NEED

TIME: One day to excavate and install about 20 feet of walkway.

SKILLS: No special skills needed.

TOOLS: Round-point shovel, drill, circular saw, handsaw, small sledgehammer, tamper.

AVAILABLE MATERIALS

- Organic materials include pine bark nuggets, chipped wood, finely shredded redwood bark (called gorilla hair), and cypress mulch. These scatter easily but won't damage your yard or be a mowing hazard.
- Large stones, such as limestone and granite, or smooth pebbles stay in place, but they make a poor walking surface and are awkward for wheels.
- Decomposed granite and crushed rock are available in small sizes. These pack tightly if you tamp them well. Redrock, composed of clay, sand, and soil, compacts well, but may decompose and blow away in prolonged dry weather.

1 EXCAVATE AND INSTALL EDGING.

After laying out the pathway, dig deep enough so your edging protrudes 1 or 2 inches above ground level. Be sure to remove organic material, especially tree roots. To construct a border of pressure-treated 4×4s, lay about 1 inch of gravel or sand in the excavation to provide drainage away from the wood. Cut the timbers with a circular saw. Place the 4×4s, making sure they are at the correct height and are stable. Level them, or where there's a slope, position them at a consistent incline. To secure the timbers, drill ⅜- or ½-inch holes through them every 2 or 3 feet and drive 2-foot-long pieces of rebar (many home centers sell these precut) through the timbers and into the ground.

2 LAY THE LOOSE MATERIAL.

Lay landscaping fabric between the 4×4s to inhibit weed growth through the path. Add 1 inch of coarse sand and tamp it level. Add the loose material of your choice. For fine material lay only 1 inch at a time, tamp or roll it firm, then add more layers until the material is 1–2 inches below the top of the edging. Backfill behind the edging and lay sod or reseed the grass.

INSTALLING STONE ON A SLAB

A mortared stone-veneer surface is beautiful and long-lasting, and needs almost no maintenance. With this approach a garden-variety walkway or patio slab can be improved dramatically at relatively low cost. Any stone veneer ¾ inch thick or less must be installed on a solid concrete surface. If the slab is not smooth, level it with concrete patch first because it is difficult to level a veneer surface as you apply it. (If you need to lay a slab, see pages 24–31 and 40–45.)

YOU'LL NEED

TIME: About one day to install 100 square feet of veneer; a few hours the next day to grout it.

SKILLS: Cutting stone.

TOOLS: Straightedge, large-notched trowel, rented wet saw, hammer, masonry chisel, rubber mallet, grout float, towels, sponges.

1 INSTALL OR PATCH CONCRETE BASE.

The base for your stone veneer must be solid. If it shifts or buckles, the veneer will crack. The slab should be at least 2 inches of concrete over a sand base. Use a straightedge to make sure it is level. Fill in low spots with patching concrete. Knock off high spots with a hammer and masonry chisel.

2 DRY-LAY THE PIECES.

If you are using irregular-shaped stones, dry-lay the pieces on the surface in the pattern you want before you mix mortar. Maintain consistent joint spacing and avoid placing small pieces along the edges. Once you've laid out about a 16-square-foot section, set aside the pieces, being careful to preserve the pattern.

3 MARK AND CUT.

When you need to cut an irregular piece for a clean fit, mark the cut line on the stone by holding it on top of the adjacent piece. See page 67 for directions on cutting stone.

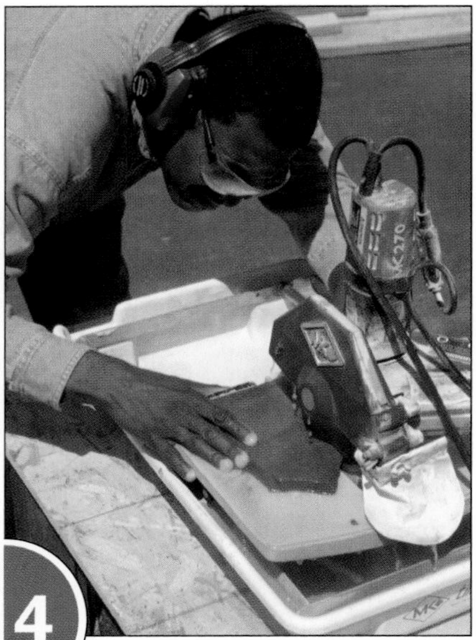

4 USE A WET SAW.

For thicker stone or to cut inside corners accurately, rent a wet saw. The saw continuously pumps water from the tray onto the blade to keep it from wearing. It cleanly slices through the hardest of materials, even granite.

APPLY THE MORTAR.

Use a thick mortar to help even the surface for the stones. Mix the mortar, allow it to set for about 10 minutes, then mix it again.

Apply the mortar in two steps: Trowel on a smooth base coating about ½ inch thick. Then go over the surface with a large-notched trowel, taking care that the notches do not penetrate through to the concrete base. Use long, sweeping strokes as you apply a second coat.

LAY THE VENEER.

Lay the stone in the pattern you dry-laid. Use spacers or eyeball the joints to make sure they're even. Use a rubber mallet to gently tap pieces into alignment.

GROUT THE JOINTS.

Allow time for the mortar to set (usually one or two days). Mix the grout of your choice, using a latex additive to help prevent cracking later. Push the grout into the joints with a grout float, making sure you move the float in at least two directions at all points. Once you are sure the joints in a small section are packed fully, scrape with the float held nearly perpendicular to the tiles to remove as much waste as possible. Clean the grout from the veneer surface and make smooth grout lines, first by laying a wet towel on the surface and pulling it toward you, then by wiping carefully with a damp sponge. Sponge-clean the surface several times.

INSTALLING TILE ON A SLAB

A mortared tile surface is an alternative to the stone veneer surface applied in the project shown on pages 72–73. Tile is just as long-lasting and low maintenance as stone but creates a more precise finish. It is a relatively low-cost way to improve a standard walk or concrete slab. Study the other materials used in your landscape and consider whether tile will coordinate with the look of your home and yard.

Select tiles for patios, porches, and walkways that have a nonslip surface. Vitreous and impervious tiles absorb the least amount of water, making them better able to withstand freezing weather. In regions with a varied climate, all of the setting materials must be labeled as freeze/thaw stable for installations in cold climates.

Any tile ¾ inch thick or less must be installed on a solid concrete surface. If the slab is not smooth, level it with concrete patch first because it is difficult to level a veneer surface as you apply it. (If you need to lay a slab, see pages 24–31 and pages 40–45.)

YOU'LL NEED

TIME: About one day to install 100 square feet of veneer; a few hours the next day to grout it.

SKILLS: Cutting tile.

TOOLS: Straightedge, large-notched trowel, tile cutter, rented wet saw, hammer, masonry chisel, rubber mallet, grout float, towels, sponges.

1 INSTALL OR PATCH CONCRETE BASE.

The base for a tile surface must be solid. If it shifts or buckles, the veneer will crack. The slab should be at least 2 inches of concrete over a sand base. Use a straightedge to make sure it is level. Fill in low spots with patching concrete. Knock off high spots with a hammer and cold chisel.

2 DRY-LAY THE PIECES.

Dry-lay the tiles on the surface in the pattern you want before you mix mortar. See page 60 for pattern options that could work with most styles of tile veneer. Maintain consistent joint spacing and avoid having to place small pieces along the edge. Once you've laid out about a 16-square-foot section, set aside the pieces, being careful to preserve the pattern.

3 MARK AND CUT.

When you need to cut a tile for a clean fit, mark the cut line on the tile by holding it on top of the adjacent piece. An inexpensive tile cutter works well for straight cuts on most types of tile. It has a guide that can be screwed in place to cut a series of tiles the same size.

4 USE A WET SAW.

If you have many tiles to cut, or for the cleanest, most accurate cuts, rent a wet saw.

5 APPLY THE MORTAR.

Use thinset mortar with a latex additive, available in both liquid and powder form. Mix the mortar, allow it to set for about 10 minutes, then mix it again.

Apply the mortar in two steps. Trowel on a smooth base coating about ½ inch thick. Then go over the surface with a large-notched trowel, taking care that the notches do not penetrate through to the concrete base. Use long, sweeping strokes as you apply a second coat.

CHOOSING AND SPACING TILES

- Do not use wall tiles for a floor or patio surface or you will end up with hairline cracks in a few years.
- Glazed tiles come in many colors, but they will be extremely slippery when wet. Use them only for accent or border pieces.
- Cut slate or quarry tiles are good choices for outdoor walks.
- If you're new to laying tiles, purchase a bag or two of plastic spacers, which slip between the tiles to maintain even grout lines. Once the mortar is set, remove the edge spacers before applying grout.

6 LAY THE VENEER.

Place each tile piece straight down so you do not have to slide it into position. Use spacers or eyeball the joints after setting every few tiles to make sure they're even. If tiles are not flush, use a flat piece of lumber wrapped in carpet and a rubber mallet to gently tap them into alignment.

7 GROUT THE JOINTS.

Allow time for the mortar to set (usually one or two days). Mix the grout of your choice, using a latex additive to keep it from cracking later. Push the grout into the joints with a grout float, making sure you move the float in at least two directions at all points. Once you are sure the joints in a small section are packed fully, scrape with the float held nearly perpendicular to the tiles to remove as much waste as possible. Clean the grout from the veneer surface and make smooth grout lines, first by laying a wet towel on the surface and pulling it toward you, then by wiping carefully with a damp sponge. Sponge-clean the surface several times.

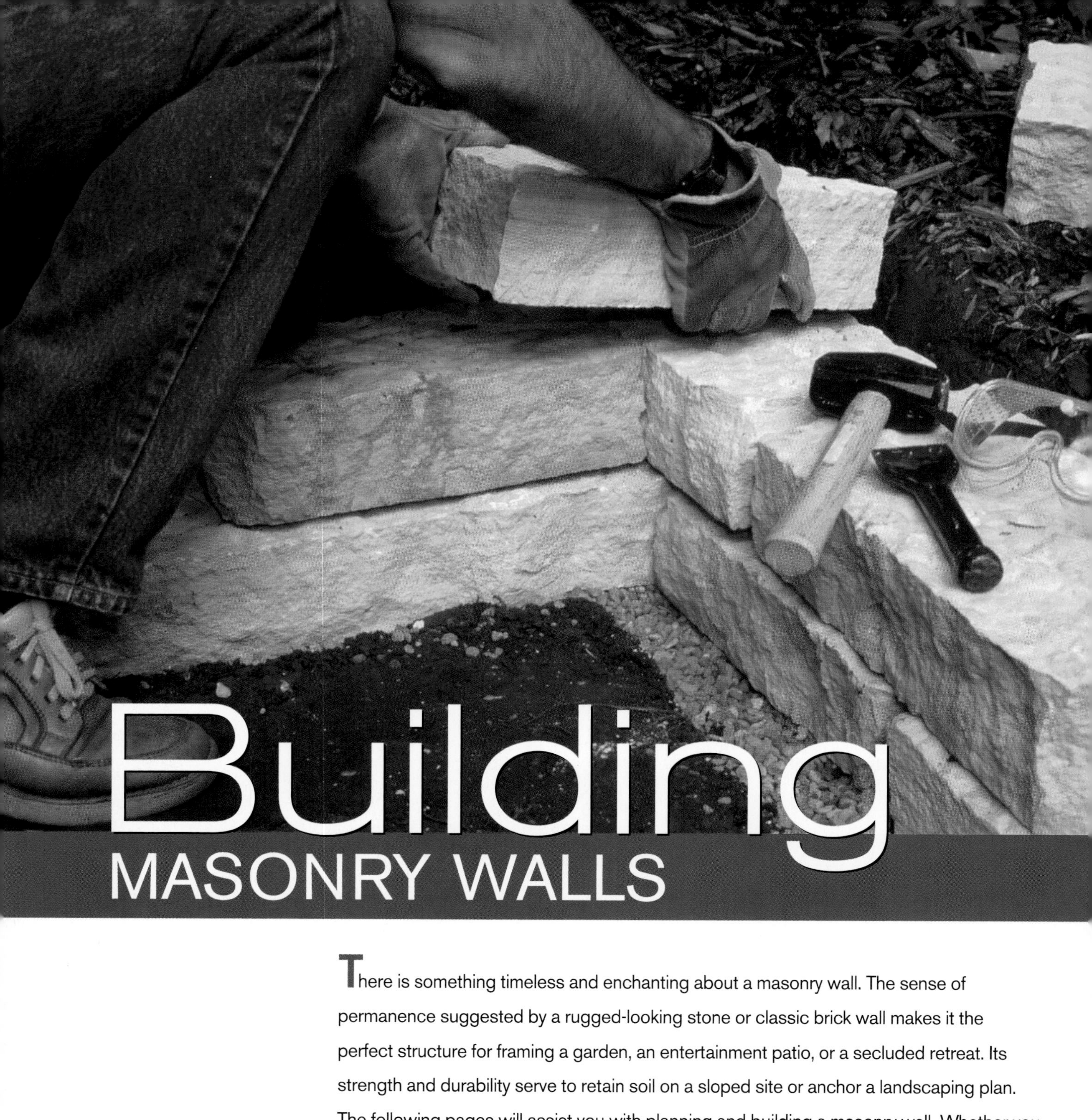

Building MASONRY WALLS

There is something timeless and enchanting about a masonry wall. The sense of permanence suggested by a rugged-looking stone or classic brick wall makes it the perfect structure for framing a garden, an entertainment patio, or a secluded retreat. Its strength and durability serve to retain soil on a sloped site or anchor a landscaping plan. The following pages will assist you with planning and building a masonry wall. Whether you wish to install a dry-laid, freestanding wall (pages 82–87) or build a mortared wall (pages 88–98), you'll find the ideas and instructions you need to make the project a success. You will also find sections on brick veneer (pages 99–102 and 104), applying stucco (pages 106–108), installing glass-block walls (page 109), and building a garden wall (page 103).

DECORATIVE BACKDROP
Brick offers a great look for decorative walls (see page 98). Here it creates a textured and visually interesting background for fountains, plants, and artifacts.

BUILDING A WALL
Stacked-stone walls add scale and texture to any landscape and fit into almost any natural setting. Flat, rectangular stones work best for producing a tight-fitting, sturdy, freestanding wall.

SIDING STYLE
On this charming home, brick veneer offsets the horizontal lines of the lap siding. See page 99 to learn about installing brick veneer.

SMOOTH LINES
The smooth lines of this stone wall establish a boundary and complement the clean lines of the home and landscape. Consider integrating plants into your design to add warmth and soften the look of a stone wall.

<
STACKED STONE
This stacked-stone wall brings structure to the garden. The flat surfaces of the stones make for a tight fit, adding strength to the wall.

^
A SPOT FOR PLANTS
A low brick wall provides a raised spot to place foundation plantings. The large, rectangular stepping-stones lead visitors to the warm richness of the patio and stoop. In such a small area, using the same material for the low wall, stepping-stones, patio, and steps provides visual continuity.

WATER AND WALLS

A retaining wall holds back a tremendous amount of soil and the water within it. The spaces between the stones in a dry-laid, freestanding wall permit water to drain through, relieving water pressure buildup that would topple some walls.

A TOUCH OF ELEGANCE

The low brick wall at the front of this property neatly defines the border of the yard and creates a spot for two majestic lion sculptures to welcome guests.

<
EMBELLISH A WALL
Raised details embellish a stucco wall, adding visual character to what otherwise would be a uniform surface. Setting molds into the wall and coating them with stucco produced this chevron design.

>
STYLE AND FUNCTION
Attractive stone-block planter boxes show off bright annuals while supporting the pergola and trellis.

A NOD TO THE PAST

Using salvaged material can bring a sense of old world charm to the landscape. Here the rustic steps are blended with smooth pavers on the walkway, adding uniqueness and depth to the entrance and establishing the theme of the space.

STYLISH STUCCO

Stucco is a period-appropriate finish for bungalows such as this one. Stucco is also a popular choice for curved walls and Southwestern architectural styles. For information about applying stucco, turn to page 106.

BUILDING DRY-LAID FREESTANDING WALLS

Building a wall of natural stone is hard work, and stone can be expensive. But the results are enduring and strikingly beautiful. Dry-laid stone walls rely on gravity, rather than mortar, to hold them together. As a result they are more difficult to build than mortared walls because you spend more time getting stones to fit well and rest solidly on each other. Don't try to build a dry-laid stone wall more than 3 feet high; it is difficult to keep it stable.

YOU'LL NEED

TIME: With stones at the site, about a day to build a wall 3 feet high and 10 feet long.

SKILLS: Cutting stones.

TOOLS: Round-point shovel, brick hammer, mason's line.

1 DIG A TRENCH AND BEGIN LAYING THE STONES.

Drive stakes and stretch mason's lines to establish the long outside edges of the wall. Remove sod, any roots larger than ½ inch in diameter, and 2 or 3 inches of soil to provide a smooth, level base. Dig the trench deep enough so the top of the first course of stones is slightly above grade.

Begin placing stones securely into the soil. Lay the stones in each course perpendicular to those in the course below. This helps tie the courses together and strengthen the wall.

USING A FOOTING

If your area is subject to frost, a stone wall will rise and fall an inch or so every year because of frost heave. Even in warm climates the weight of the stones will make a wall settle. As long as the wall is not cemented together with mortar, this is not a problem. The stones will move a bit in relation to each other, and you may have to refit a stone or two over the years. But if the stones are placed well to begin with, the wall should remain solid. You can cement the stones together with mortar; however, that requires a footing, dug below the frost line, to keep the mortar from cracking.

2 FILL IN GAPS.

Fill voids in the center of the wall with small stones and plug vertical gaps between stones by tapping chinks (small pieces of stone) into place. Cut these chinks and any other small stones as needed with a brick hammer. Wear eye and hand protection when breaking stones. Always avoid placing stones of the same size directly on top of each other.

3 TOP OFF WITH CAPSTONES.

Build the wall so it becomes slightly narrower as it rises. This makes the wall more stable. Notice in the wall pictured here how the stones form bonds both across the width and along the length of the wall. Some masons spread mortar over the stones in the next-to-top course, then set the capstones into the mortar. This helps seal the top of the wall from moisture.

CAUTION

WATCH YOUR BACK

Working with stone can be, almost literally, backbreaking work. Have a strong-backed helper on hand and lift the heavy stones together. Lift with your legs, keeping your back straight and upright to avoid strain. Take frequent breaks and do not work more than a few hours a day if you are not used to this kind of labor.

CHECK LOCAL CODES

In many localities, building codes also apply to stone walls, especially if they are used as retaining walls. Before you begin, check with your building department and follow their instructions.

BUILDING DRY-LAID RETAINING WALLS

The basics of building a retaining wall are similar to those for a free-standing wall. The main difference is that you should excavate the hillside and provide drainage.

Before building the wall, you need to cut and fill the grade. Wrap the gravel and drainpipe in landscaping fabric to filter out loose soil that might clog the system.

If the soil you want to retain is more than 4 feet high, do not attempt to hold it back with one dry-laid stone wall. Build steplike terraces instead.

YOU'LL NEED

TIME: For a 10-foot-long and 3-foot-high wall, about a day to excavate and provide drainage and two days to build the wall.

SKILLS: Digging, cutting stone.

TOOLS: Round-point shovel, brick hammer, brick set, small sledgehammer, mason's line.

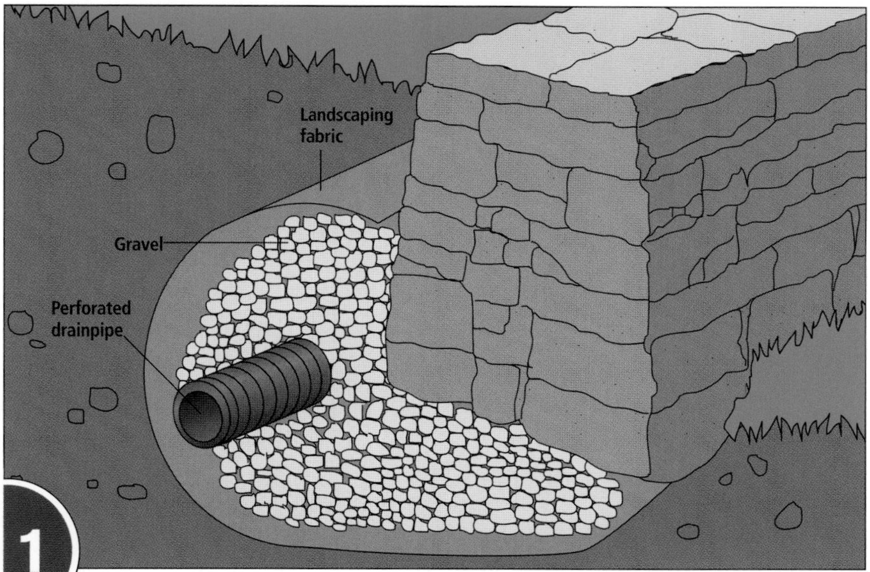

1 EXCAVATE AND PROVIDE DRAINAGE.

Dig into the hill you want to retain to excavate a base for the wall. On the hill side of the wall, dig a drainage ditch. Lay down landscaping fabric and gravel and set perforated drainpipe on the gravel, making sure the pipe slopes slightly toward a spot where you want excess water to flow. Cover the drainpipe with gravel and landscaping fabric.

Build the wall as you would a dry stone wall. Be sure, however, to slope it slightly toward the hill that is being retained.

Building dry-laid retaining walls *(continued)*

2 EXCAVATE AND LAY FIRST COURSE.

After staking and laying out the front perimeter, level an area for the wall and lay the first course. If a stone is loose as you place it, trowel some soil under and around it to stabilize it.

3 CUT STONES TO FIT.

Lay subsequent courses carefully, experimenting with different stones and making adjustments so they sit solidly on each other. To cut large stones to fit, score a line all the way around, about ⅛ inch deep, using a brick set. Be sure to wear gloves and eye protection as you work. Place the stone on a solid support along the score line and hit the unsupported part with firm strokes from a small sledgehammer until the stone splits in two.

4 INSTALL TIE STONES.

As you build the wall, avoid placing stones such that joints line up vertically. Use long stones that span two or more joints whenever possible. Be sure every stone rests solidly in place or it may work loose later.

Slope the face of the retaining wall 10 to 20 degrees from vertical so it leans toward the backfill it is to retain. Use a batter guide (see page 88–89). To keep the middle of the wall from bulging, install long tie stones about every 4 feet, halfway up the wall.

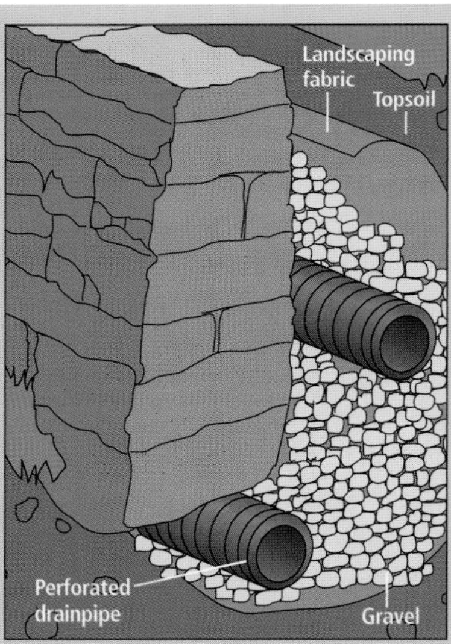

ADD MORE DRAINPIPE WHERE NEEDED.

For severe drainage problems, use two pipes. Behind the wall lay gravel on landscaping fabric, then place drainpipe on the gravel bed and cover it with more gravel. Wrap the fabric around the gravel bed and cover it with more gravel.

BUILDING SHORT FLAGSTONE WALLS

A short flagstone wall is easy to build because it does not require a drainage system or a footing and can be constructed with light flagstones. This type of wall can be used where you do not need to retain large amounts of soil, such as a flower bed. Usually it is best if the wall is no more than 3 feet high. During a heavy rain, water will seep through the face of the wall.

YOU'LL NEED

TIME: About one day to build a wall 3 feet high by 15 feet long.

SKILLS: Laying stone.

TOOLS: Round-point shovel, rake, brick set, small sledgehammer, brick trowel.

1 CUT AND FILL.

Dig a trench about 10 inches deep and 1 foot wider than the wall. Remove or add dirt to the hill behind the wall so it slopes toward the wall about 1 inch per rising foot. Maintain the same slope across the length of the wall. Fill the trench with gravel and rake it smooth and level with the adjoining ground surface.

2 LAY THE STONES.

Lay the first course using large stones so they span the gravel bed. As you lay succeeding courses, stagger the joints and be sure each stone rests solidly, without wobbling. Save smaller stones for the upper courses, but keep some large flagstones for the top course. Batter the wall toward the hill.

You can leave the joints in the wall bare, or you can mix soil with a small amount of water to achieve a mortar-like consistency. Press the mixture into gaps in the wall. In time, small plants or grass will grow there, lending a rustic, mature appearance to the wall.

3 MORTAR THE TOP COURSE.

This optional step makes a wall stronger. Dry-fit the top course in a pleasing pattern, then remove the stones and place them adjacent to the wall so you can remember where they go. Mix and apply a 2-inch layer of mortar on the next-to-last course and lay the top stones. You may need to fill in some gaps with small stones.

BUILDING INTERLOCKING-BLOCK WALLS

Interlocking block retaining walls are a cost-effective and durable choice for preventing the natural erosion of soil or transforming the landscape of your yard. They are easy to construct and can accommodate many different preferences as they come in a variety of colors, sizes, shapes, and textures. Some manufacturers make blocks that allow you to fill them with soil and plant small flowering plants in them. It is important to prepare the foundation for the wall properly. Before building the wall, you need to cut and fill the grade (see page 85.) Wrap the gravel and drainpipe in landscaping fabric to filter out loose soil that might clog the system.

YOU'LL NEED

TIME: For a 10-foot-long and 3-foot-high wall, about a day to excavate and provide drainage, and a day to build the wall.

SKILLS: Cutting blocks.

TOOLS: Round-point shovel, trowel, brick hammer, brick set, small sledgehammer, rubber mallet, line level, carpenter's level, mason's line, tamper.

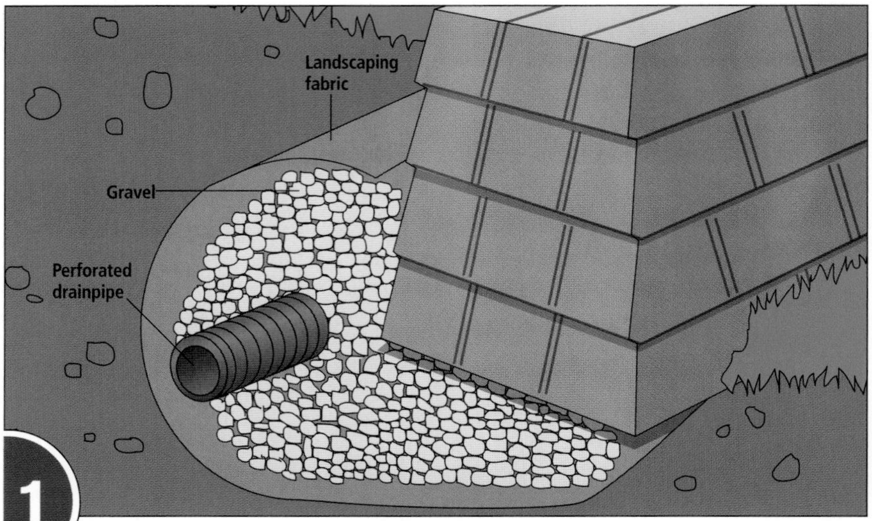

1 EXCAVATE AND PROVIDE DRAINAGE.

The first course of blocks should be below ground level. A good guideline is to bury the base row 1 inch below the surface for every 8 inches of height above the ground. For larger projects, installing drainage will relieve pressure on the wall. Dig into the hill you want to retain and prepare a base for the wall. On the hill side of the wall, dig a drainage ditch. Place landscaping fabric and gravel. Set perforated drainpipe on the gravel, making sure the pipe slopes slightly toward a spot where you want excess water to flow. Cover the drainpipe with gravel and landscaping fabric. Compact the fill with a 4×4 or hand tamper. Check for level using a carpenter's level.

2 PREPARE FOR THE BASE ROW.

The first row of blocks establishes the shape of the project. Therefore it is important to make sure you have a solid base and that the first row is level. Place stakes at both ends of the wall. Tie a mason's line between them, and using a line level, set the line for the top of the first course.

3 SET THE BLOCKS.

If you need to make adjustments to the height of a block, either remove fill below the block or tap it down using a rubber mallet. If a block is loose as you place it, trowel some fill material under and around it to stabilize it. Set each block so its edge touches the adjacent block.

4 CHECK FOR LEVEL.

Level the row in both directions. Use a carpenter's level for the length of the row and to make sure the blocks are level front to back.

5 BACKFILL EACH ROW.

As you finish each row of a wall, backfill behind and between the blocks. Use dirt for backfill for small walls and crushed stone or river rock for walls greater than three rows in height. Compact the backfill using a tamper. Clean the top of each row before you start setting the next row. Adjust the mason's line height for the top of the next row.

6 INTERLOCK EACH ROW.

Each row will lock to the row beneath it. Some styles of interlocking blocks have a flange on the lower back edge to lock onto the lower row. Others have holes in the top and bottom for pins to lock the rows in place. With flange-type interlocking blocks, you may need to make a correction for a tighter curve. This may require knocking off part or all of the flange with a hammer. Just remember that doing so will create a weak link in the wall.

7 CUT BLOCKS TO FIT.

Lay subsequent courses carefully, making adjustments so the blocks sit solidly on each other. See page 67 for how to mark and cut blocks with a brick hammer. Be sure to wear gloves and safety goggles as you work. Place the block on a solid support along the score line and hit the unsupported part with firm strokes from a small sledgehammer until the block splits in two.

8 SET THE CAP TO FINISH.

Though not necessary, you may wish to top the wall with capstones. This provides a professional finish and gives you the option of mixing in different material styles and colors to set off the wall. If using a pin-type block, you'll need a special "cap" block for the top row.

BUILDING MORTARED STONE WALLS

Choose stones that blend well together, both in color and texture. Using a good variety of sizes not only looks better but also makes it less likely you'll have to cut stones. Ashlar (square-hewn stone) is best to work with, but semidressed stone or rubble works well also. Have the stones delivered as close to your work site as possible to minimize lifting. Be prepared for some difficult physical labor. You'll have to lift, shift, and try different stones to get the best fit.

YOU'LL NEED

TIME: 1 day to pour the footing and 2 days to build a wall 4 feet high and 10 feet long.

SKILLS: Excavating, pouring and finishing concrete, cutting stone, cutting lumber.

TOOLS: Round-point shovel, tamper, mortar box and hoe, drill or hammer, mason's line, brick trowel, wedges, brush.

WORKING WITH MORTAR

Don't allow excess or smeared mortar to dry and set on the stones. Every stone or two, take the time to wipe the stones clean with a wet rag. It is much harder to remove excess mortar once it sets.

Because stones are not as porous as bricks or blocks, they do not absorb much moisture and mortar sets up more slowly. If mortar squeezes out quickly, sprinkle on a bit more mortar mix or portland cement to absorb water and stiffen the mortar before setting on a stone.

1 LAY A CONCRETE FOUNDATION.

Unlike a dry stone wall, a mortared wall develops ugly cracks if it settles unevenly. Dig a trench about 6 inches wider than the wall and 6 inches deeper than the frost line (at least 12 inches deep). Tamp at least 2 inches of gravel at the bottom, position two pieces of reinforcing bar, and pour at least 8 inches of concrete. Finish the concrete footing so it's 2 inches below grade.

2 MAKE BATTER GUIDES.

Build two batter guides out of 1×4 lumber; use these to make sure your wall batters, or slopes inward, about 1 inch per rising foot on both sides.

3 LAY THE FIRST COURSE.

Allow the concrete foundation to set and cure for several days. Spread a 2-inch-thick bed of mortar. Start on the end with a tie stone—a stone that spans the width of the wall. Use large stones along the visible face of the wall and fill in the middle with smaller stones and mortar. Tap the stones with the handle of your trowel to force air pockets out of the mortar.

4 LAY THE STONES.

Build up the ends, called leads, first. Position the batter guides at each end of the wall and use mason's lines to make sure you maintain a uniform slope and line up the stones straight. Dry-fit several stones, remove them, place the mortar, then set the stones in position. Place tie stones about every 4 feet in alternating positions for each succeeding course. If a heavy stone squeezes out too much mortar, use wood wedges to support the stones until the mortar sets. Maintain uniform joint spacing.

5 RAKE THE JOINTS.

As you complete a section of wall, use a piece of shim or a scrap of wood to scrape away mortar to a depth of about 1 inch. Follow with a stiff brush and a wet rag if necessary to make sure the stones are clean and the joints are uniform.

6 BUILD SECOND LEAD, FILL IN THE MIDDLE, AND TOP WITH CAPSTONES.

Use flat, smooth stones for the visible ends of the wall. Lay no more than three courses of stones per day; lay more than that and the weight of the stones will squeeze mortar out of the bottom courses.

Fill in the middle section, again dry-fitting the stones, removing them, laying on plenty of mortar, and carefully setting the stones in the mortar. Don't forget to include tie stones in every other course, every 4 feet or so.

Cap off the wall with a row of large, flat stones. When you mortar these stones on top of the wall, do not rake the joints. Brush them flush with the surface of the capstones to keep water from sitting in the joints, freezing, and damaging the wall.

BUILDING CONCRETE-BLOCK WALLS

Laying concrete blocks is hard, physical labor. Not only will you be lifting 40-pound blocks all day long, but often you'll be handling them in awkward positions. There's mortar to be mixed and transported, which involves plenty of heavy lifting as well, so have plenty of strong help. Professionals work in fairly large crews, so don't expect to do this project alone.

YOU'LL NEED

TIME: With a helper, at least a full day for a 10×8-foot wall.

SKILLS: Laying straight courses, checking for plumb, throwing mortar, checking course height.

TOOLS: Chalk line, mason's line, plumb bob, story pole or modular spacing rule, carpenter's level, small sledgehammer, pointed trowel, brick set, circular saw with masonry blade, pointing trowel, brush.

TIPS FOR BUILDING A CONCRETE-BLOCK WALL

- A solid footing or foundation is essential to building a concrete-block wall. Check local building codes, and follow the instructions on pages 28–31.
- Choose a Type "S" or "M" mortar. Both are strong and resistant to damage from freezing.
- Use true concrete blocks, which weigh 40 pounds or more, rather than lightweight cinder blocks. Concrete block is stronger and more moisture-resistant; it's worth the expense.

1 ESTABLISH THE CORNERS.

If your project involves just one wall, skip Steps 1 and 2. Determine the two end points of the wall and snap a chalk line on the footing to designate the edge of the wall. Go on to Step 3.

Mark the locations of the corners. Stretch a mason's line between the batter boards you set up before excavating for the footing, placing the line on the mark for the outside of the wall (see pages 28–29). Have a helper dangle a plumb bob from the point at which the mason's lines intersect at each corner, taking care not to disturb their alignment. Mark the locations on the footings with a thick pencil.

2 MARK FOR THE WALLS.

Sweep the footings clean and snap chalk lines between the corner marks. Check the lines for square, using the 3-4-5 method described on page 25.

3 LAY THE BOTTOM MORTAR.

Make sure the footing is still clean and lay a 1-inch bed of mortar for the first course of blocks. Start at a corner, running the length of two or three blocks. Make the bed of mortar at least 1 inch wider than the blocks you'll be placing.

4 SET THE CORNER BLOCK.

Dampen blocks slightly to prevent rapid moisture loss from the mortar. Carefully place a corner block in position, with the smaller holes in its cores facing up and its smooth-faced, solid end on the corner. Gently press the block into place in the mortar.

5 MEASURE THE BLOCK HEIGHT WITH A STORY POLE...

Use a story pole to check for proper course height. To make a story pole, choose a straight 2×4 and make clear perpendicular marks every 8 inches. As you add the courses, the top of each concrete block should align with one of the marks. If the block is too high, tap it down into the mortar with the trowel handle. If it's too low, pull the block out, place more mortar on the bed, and re-lay the block.

OR USE A FOLDING OR MODULAR SPACING RULE.

If you use a conventional folding rule or tape measure, the top of the block should be 8 inches above the footing. Confirm that the mortar joint under the block is exactly ⅜ inch thick. On a modular spacing rule (see inset) the top of the block should match the line at the "2."

Building concrete-block walls *(continued)*

6 BUTTER AND LAY THE NEXT BLOCKS.

Before laying the second block, butter its flanges (or ears) while it is standing on end. Butter it well because this mortar forms the vertical joint between the first and second blocks. Set the block in place, making sure you have a ⅜-inch joint spacing. Repeat with subsequent blocks.

7 CHECK FOR LEVEL AND PLUMB.

Place a level along the length of the first three blocks. If they are not perfectly level or if their tops do not form a straight line, press or tap down on the high points until they are level.

Check for plumb by holding the level against the side of each block. If any block is not plumb, press with the heel of your hand or tap with the handle of your trowel to adjust it.

Every three or four blocks, check for level and plumb and make adjustments. Periodically use your level or a long straightedge to make sure the faces of the blocks align.

8 CHECK FOR SQUARE AND BUILD LEAD.

Check corners for square first by holding a framing square against the outside edges of each side. Then use the 3-4-5 method as a double-check (see page 25).

Apply a 1-inch-deep layer of mortar along the top edges of the blocks of the first course. As you place the second corner block, align its outside corner with the corner below it. Press the block into the mortar just enough so its weight compresses the mortar to a ⅜-inch joint. Continue laying blocks until you have built up a corner lead.

WHY BUILD CORNER LEADS?

Whenever you build a masonry wall, whether it's with bricks, blocks, or stones, it is best to start by building leads at each corner. Then you can fill in blocks between the leads. You may be tempted to skip this step and build a wall one course at a time. But leads are essential to achieve a plumb and straight wall. Without leads you have to check blocks continually for level and plumb, and there would be no easy way to make sure your wall is straight. With the leads in place, laying the blocks in the middle is simple: stretch a mason's line from corner to corner and follow it.

9 INSTALL SPACERS IF NECESSARY.

Spacers made of cut blocks can be used to extend leads if you cannot make the number of blocks come out even by slightly enlarging the mortar lines. Cut and install spacer blocks early, rather than trying to cut the closure block in the middle to fit.

10 CUT CONCRETE BLOCKS BY HAND...

If you need to cut blocks to fit, be sure to take into account the ⅜-inch mortar lines when measuring. To cut by hand, place the block on sand or loose soil and use a brick set and hammer to make a line about ⅛ inch deep on both sides of the block. Then work along the line again, hammering harder and moving the brick set each time you rap it. Continue until the block breaks along the cut line.

OR WITH A SAW.

For precision cuts use a circular saw with a diamond or masonry cutting blade. Be sure the block is dry when you cut it.

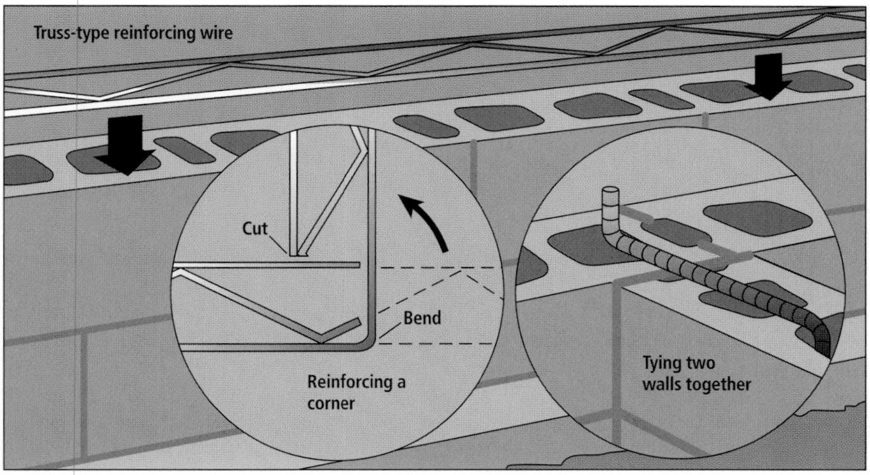

ADD REINFORCING WIRE WHEN NEEDED.

For retaining walls and foundation walls on which there will be considerable lateral pressure, beef up the wall with truss-type or ladder-type reinforcing wire. Embed the wire in the mortar of every other horizontal joint. As you embed it, overlay the ends of the sections by at least 6 inches.

The left inset shows how to position the wire when reinforcing a corner. Cut two of the wires in the truss and bend the remaining one to form the corner.

The right inset shows how to tie intersecting walls together with an S-shaped, ⅜-inch rebar. Once covered with mortar and the next course of blocks, the rebar is secured firmly to the webbing of the blocks.

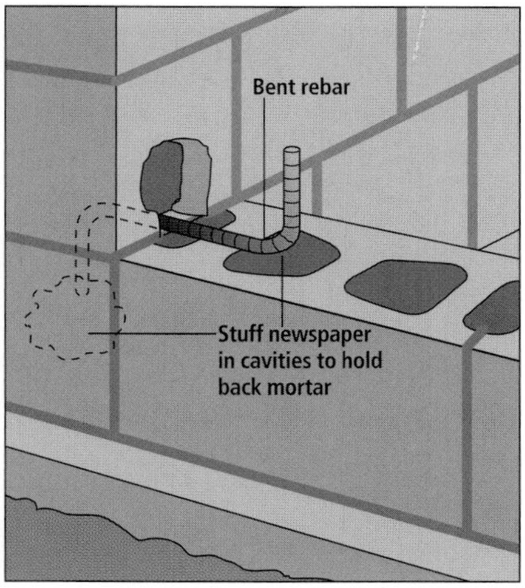

TIE A NEW WALL TO AN OLD ONE.

If you're building a new wall adjacent to an old one, tie the two together. Every other course, knock a hole through the existing wall, stuff newspaper into the cavity, and place an Z-shaped piece of rebar in the hole. Fill the hole with mortar or concrete. Stuff newspaper in the cavity under the other end of the rebar, lay the second course, and fill the cavity.

Building concrete-block walls *(continued)*

11 FILL IN BETWEEN THE LEADS.

Once you have two corner leads in place, hook line blocks around the corners and stretch a mason's line between them. Align the mason's line with the top of the blocks in the course being worked on and hold them about 1⁄16 inch away from the blocks' outer edges.

With the mason's line stretched in place, begin setting the blocks between the leads. Check the line often to make sure no blocks or mortar are touching it because they might otherwise push the line out of alignment.

12 INSTALL THE CLOSURE BLOCK.

Butter both ends of the closure, or final, block and lay it to complete the course. If some of the mortar falls off the flanges, lay the block anyway. Fill gaps in the joints by tucking mortar in place from the sides with your trowel.

13 STRIKE THE JOINTS.

Use a jointer or a sled jointer to finish each joint after you have laid two courses above it. Tool the head (vertical) joints first, then the bed (horizontal) joints. Brush off loose mortar, then restrike. For blocks below grade, strike off excess mortar with your trowel.

INSTALL WINDOW OR DOOR HEADERS.

Plan door and window openings to minimize cutting blocks to fit around them. It's best to use metal frames designed for use in masonry walls, but you can build wood frames as well. You can make your own header with two angle irons and U-blocks. Cut or purchase angle irons 16 inches longer than the opening is wide, allowing for an 8-inch overlap on either side of the opening. Set them back-to-back and place U-blocks on top.

CAP THE WALL.

If the foundation wall supports brick or stone veneer, use a combination of brick and smaller-size block as the cap, as shown here. For example, if the foundation blocks are 12 inches, stack 8-inch block and bricks on top.

If the wall serves as a foundation for a wood frame building, lay wire mesh on top of the next-to-last course of blocks. Embed anchor bolts in concrete in the cores of the top course of blocks. Once the mortar sets, drill holes in a pressure-treated sill plate, set the sill plate over the anchor bolts, and fasten it in place with washers and nuts.

APPLY STUCCO ON CONCRETE BLOCK.

To apply a stucco finish on concrete blocks, first paint the blocks with latex concrete bonding agent. Apply the scratch coat with a finishing trowel and scratch it with a plasterer's rake or a scratching tool made of a piece of 2×2 and 4-penny nails. Keep the scratch coat moist for two days, then apply a finish coat. (See pages 106–107 for detailed instructions on applying stucco.)

SURFACE-BONDED BLOCK

Special mortarless concrete blocks can form a strong wall when simply stacked on top of each other, reinforced, and grouted. This type of block, however, is expensive.

A more practical solution is to build a surface-bonded wall, which uses standard concrete blocks. With this process you mortar only the first course of blocks. Then you simply stack the rest of the blocks on top of each other. Once all the blocks are stacked, apply a coat of ready-made bonding agent made of portland cement mixed with pieces of fiberglass. The bonding material is available in many colors. The resulting wall actually is stronger than a standard mortared wall.

PLANNING BRICK WALLS

Several brick projects are included on pages 99–104: brick veneer walls, single-tier walls, garden walls, and lightweight veneers. All involve the same basic bricklaying techniques. The procedures used with bricks are similar to those used with concrete-block walls, only the scale is different (see pages 90–95). Both types of masonry walls require you to learn the art of working with mortar (see pages 88–89).

Check with your local building department for requirements regarding the type and size of materials you can use. There also may be standards for how a new wall should be attached to your house.

Make sure a new wall rests on a solid foundation. Footings must be reinforced and extend below the frost line. Generally, a footing should be twice as wide as the wall it supports and its thickness should equal the thickness of the finished wall. (See pages 28–29 and 35–36 for concrete footings and pages 90–95 for concrete-block foundation walls.) A brick-veneer wall on a house, however, doesn't necessarily need a new foundation; a solid ledge will suffice (see page 99).

Shown at right are some of the most common brick patterns—what masons refer to as bonds. Select a pattern as well as a top cap if your project requires it. In addition, choose the type of mortar joint that best suits your needs (see page 147).

Brick bond patterns

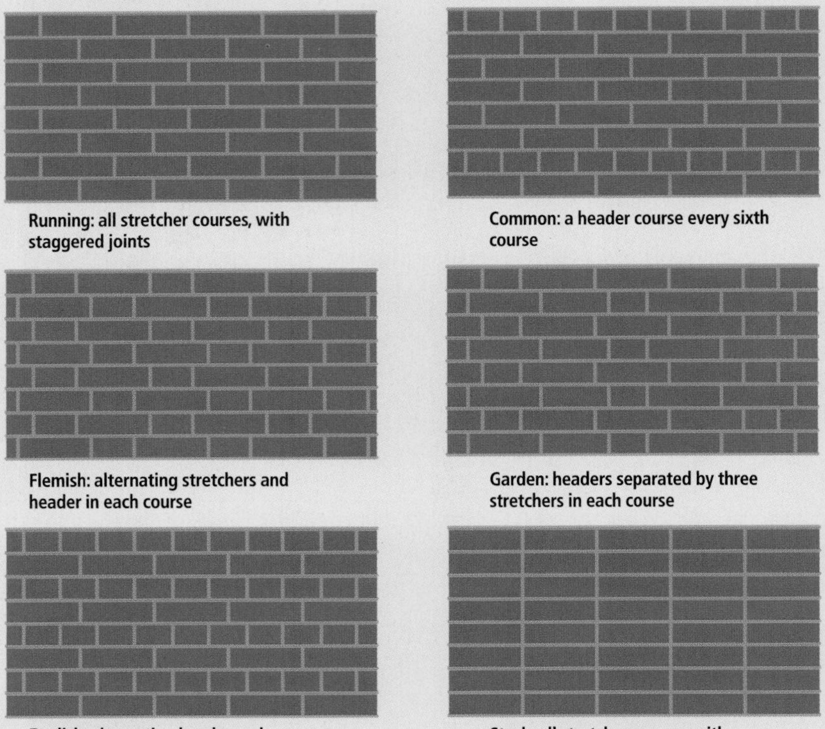

Running: all stretcher courses, with staggered joints

Common: a header course every sixth course

Flemish: alternating stretchers and header in each course

Garden: headers separated by three stretchers in each course

English: alternating header and stretcher courses

Stack: all stretcher courses with stacked joints

Top cap options

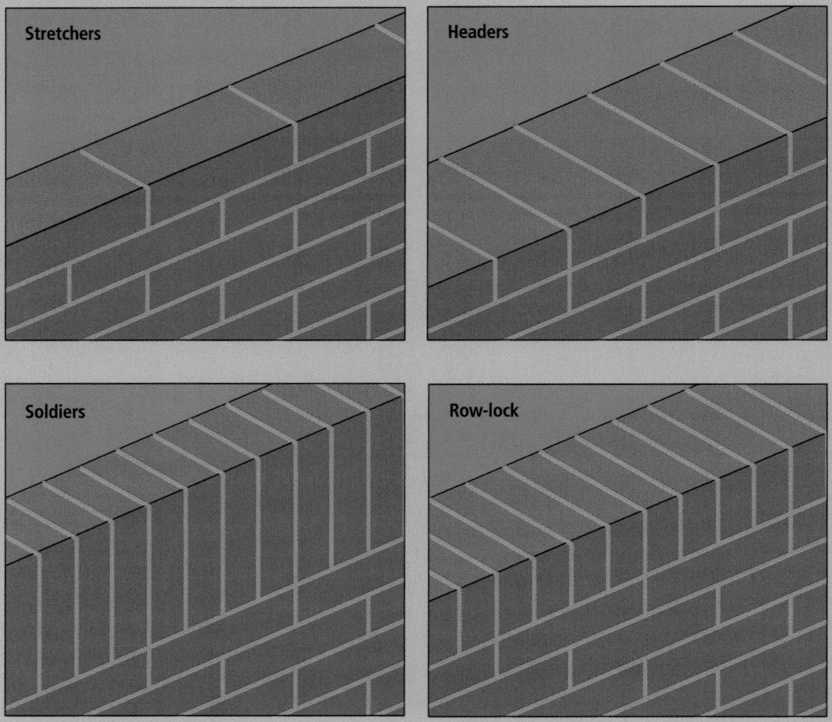

WORKING WITH MORTAR

Laying bricks in mortar requires practice to gain proficiency. You probably will never be able to throw mortar and lay bricks as quickly as a journeyman, but with patience you can learn to make straight walls with clean joints.

Professional masons take their mortar seriously. Mortar must be just the right consistency, neither soupy nor dry. It must have the correct ratio of sand, lime, and cement. Otherwise laying bricks will be a struggle and it will be difficult to keep the courses even.

For small jobs and repair work, use premixed mortar that contains sand. For larger jobs you may be able to save money by buying the sand and the cement separately and mixing them yourself.

1 MIX THE MORTAR.

Consult your supplier for the best mix for your area and your project. In most cases a good ratio is 4 parts sand, ½ part lime, and 1 part mason's cement. Adding too much lime and sand weakens the mortar. Measure by shovelfuls.

Mix small batches in a wheelbarrow; for larger jobs, use a mortar box. Shovel in half the sand, then all the mortar and lime, then the rest of the sand. Mix the dry materials thoroughly.

2 ADD COLOR PIGMENT.

If you want to color the mortar, add the pigment to your dry mix. Follow label instructions carefully. Keep accurate track of your proportions so if you mix another batch you can achieve the same color. If you retemper (remoisten) colored grout, you will change its color. So don't mix too large a batch and don't let it dry out.

3 TEST THE MORTAR.

Carefully mix in clean water a little bit at a time. Pick up a small amount of mortar with your trowel and quickly turn the trowel upside down. If the mortar sticks, it is the correct consistency. If the mortar stiffens before you use it all, add water and remix. (Don't do this with colored mortar.) But if it stiffens a second time, throw it out and make a new batch.

Working with mortar *(continued)*

4 PICK UP THE MORTAR.

Drop a shovelful of mortar onto the mortarboard. Place the mortarboard close to your work and keep it at a comfortable height so it will be easy to move mortar onto the wall.

Simply getting the mortar on your brick trowel in the correct position takes some practice. Slice off a gob and shape it so it is about the size and shape of your trowel. Scoop it up with a smooth sweep, giving a slight upward jerk with your wrist to make the mortar stick firmly to the trowel. Take the time to practice this essential technique.

5 THROW THE MORTAR.

Bricklayers talk of "throwing" mortar for a reason. Don't try to carefully place it. In one motion, flick your wrist and pull the trowel toward you. Plopping the mortar onto the bricks helps it adhere better. Using a standard-size brick trowel with the correct amount of mortar, you can throw enough mortar for two bricks.

6 FURROW THE MORTAR.

Spread the mortar to an even thickness if necessary. Lightly draw the point of the trowel across the length of the mortar to make a furrow down its middle. Don't make the furrow too deep or you may form an air pocket.

7 BUTTER THE BRICK END.

Some bricks stick better if they are dampened. Ask your supplier if this is recommended. After the corner brick is laid, butter one end of the other bricks using a scraping motion with the trowel.

8 PLACE THE BRICK, REMOVE EXCESS.

Place each brick so you have to slide it only slightly into place. Push it firmly up against the preceding brick. Immediately slice off the excess mortar oozing from the sides; use this excess as part of your next trowel load.

PREPARING WALLS FOR BRICK VENEER

Older homes often were built with double brick walls: two separate walls with a 1- or 2-inch air space between them. More common today is a single-width or brick-veneer wall that covers the face of a frame building. Although the brick wall is tied to the frame wall at various points (see page 101), there is an air space between the two. This space can be filled with insulation. Such brick is not a structural element of the house.

YOU'LL NEED

TIME: Varies considerably depending on the composition, complexity, and condition of the wall being covered.

SKILLS: Excavating and carpentry.

TOOLS: Spacing rule, shovel, hammer, level, drill with masonry bit, pry bar or other demolition tools, circular saw.

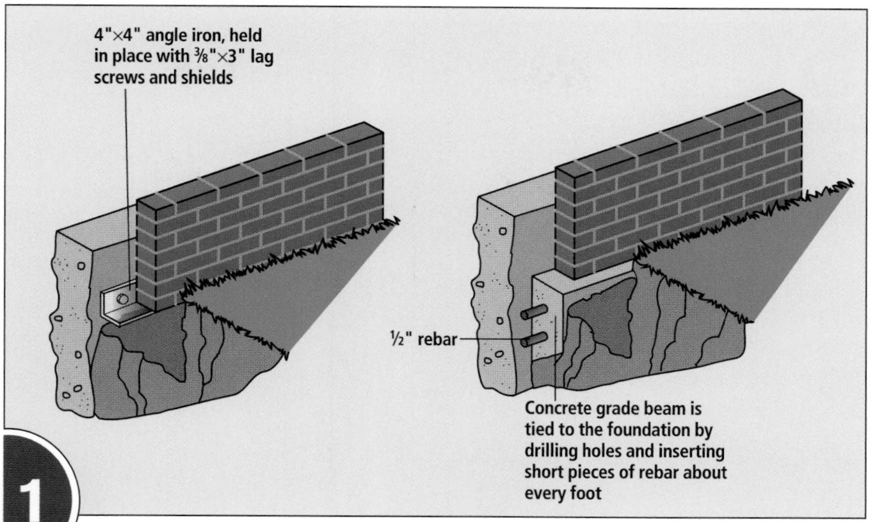

1 PROVIDE SUPPORT FOR THE BRICKS.

Excavate a trench about 1 foot deep and at least 18 inches wide along the original foundation. To support the brick veneer, use one of the methods shown, either an angle iron or a concrete grade beam. Or use a wide concrete slab or concrete-block foundation (see page 90).

If you'll be bricking around windows or doors, use a spacing rule to determine at what level the first course should be so a row-lock course of bricks can be positioned conveniently beneath the opening (see page 102).

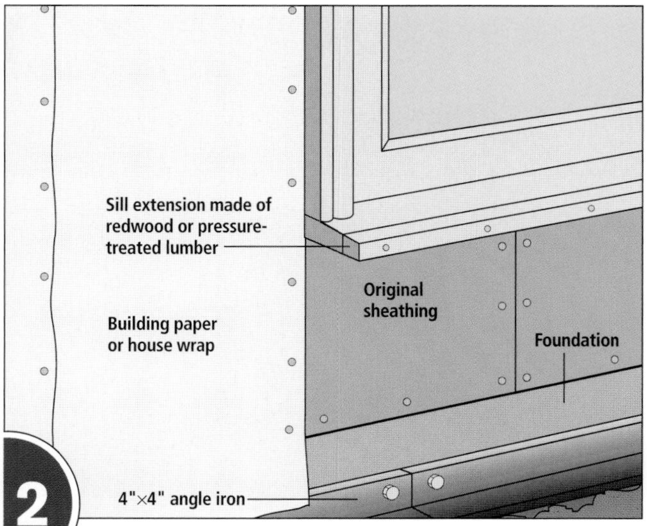

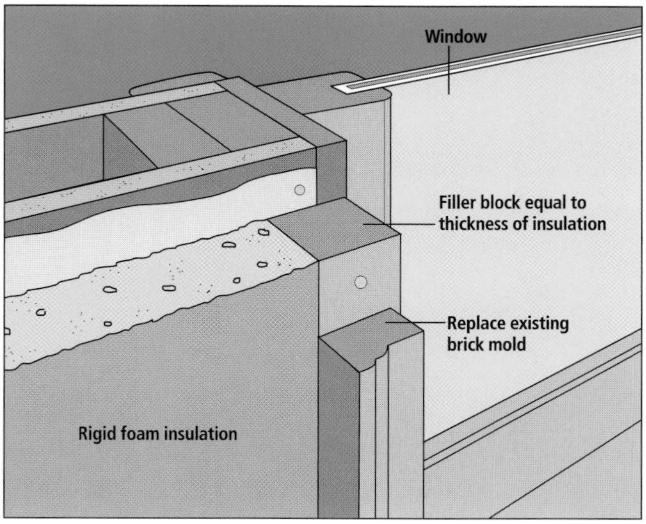

2 PREPARE THE HOUSE WALL.

Remove siding with a pry bar and cover the wall with building paper or house wrap. The paper or wrap should overlap the edge of the angle iron or grade beam. Nail redwood or pressure-treated extensions to windowsills so they reach at least ⅜ inch beyond the new veneer to facilitate drainage. If possible add 1–2 inches of rigid foam insulation between the existing wall and the new veneer. Remove window and door moldings, trim out with redwood or pressure-treated filler blocks, and reattach the molding. You may need to replace the existing molding with brick mold.

LAYING SINGLE-TIER BRICK VENEER

Single-tier brick veneer is much like siding. It serves only as an outer finished shell that functions as protection and decoration. A single-tier veneer wall supports only itself. It requires an air space between the bricks and the structure to vent moisture that builds up in the cavity. You also need a means of tying the veneer to the structure. Otherwise the bricklaying techniques are essentially the same as for any brick structure.

YOU'LL NEED

TIME: A day for an 8×10-foot wall.

SKILLS: Mixing and applying mortar, measuring and leveling, cutting bricks, striking joints.

TOOLS: Trowel, level, story pole or modular spacing rule, brick set, small sledgehammer, hammer, jointer, brush.

1 LAY A BED OF MORTAR.

Install galvanized or aluminum flashing along the base of the wall. Before you mix the mortar, dry-lay a course of bricks and make required position adjustments. Mix the mortar and sprinkle several bricks with water. On one end of the flashing, throw a 1-inch-deep bed of mortar long enough to lay two or three bricks. Furrow the bed with the tip of the trowel, as shown above. (See pages 97–98 for how to handle mortar.)

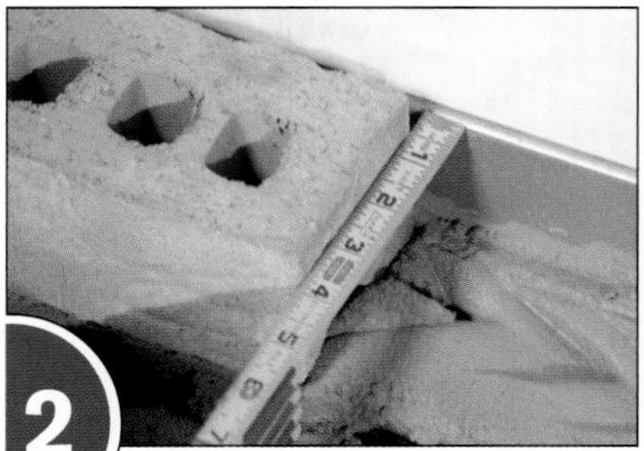

2 LAY THE FIRST BRICK.

Press the first brick into place, keeping a $\frac{1}{2}$-inch air space between it and the wall surface and a $\frac{3}{8}$-inch mortar joint beneath it. Trim excess mortar, returning it to your mortarboard or placing it farther down on the flashing.

3 MEASURE AND ALIGN AS YOU GO.

After you lay three or four bricks, measure the thickness of both the head and bed joints. They should all be $\frac{3}{8}$ inch thick. If they aren't thick enough, pull out the bricks, spread more mortar, and lay them again. Use a carpenter's level to make sure the tops are level. Check the face of each brick to make sure it is plumb. Finally lay the level horizontally along the face of the bricks (or use a mason's line and line blocks) to make sure you are building a straight wall.

4 ADD WEEP HOLES.

As you lay bricks on top of the flashing, lay short pieces of $\frac{1}{4}$-inch cord on the flashing about every 2 feet. Make sure the cords extend all the way through to the flashing. Once the mortar stiffens, pull out the cords to create weep holes. These weep holes help drain water that builds up behind the brick.

5 BUILD UP THE LEADS.

Lay a bed of mortar and continue laying brick until you have built a five- or six-course lead at each end of the wall (for more on building leads, see box below and page 94). Check your work often to make sure all the units are level, plumb, and aligned. Also check that you are maintaining a $\frac{3}{8}$-inch-thick mortar bed.

6 FILL IN THE MIDDLE.

Stretch a mason's line between the corner leads. Position line blocks (see page 128) so the mason's line aligns with and is about $\frac{1}{16}$ inch out from the top of the first course of bricks. Lay the remainder of the bricks in the first course. Mortar both ends of the last brick in the course before setting it in the mortar bed. Move the line blocks and mason's line up one course and continue laying bricks up to the mason's line.

7 ANCHOR THE BRICK VENEER.

To tie the brick veneer to the existing wall, nail brick ties every 32 inches horizontally and 16 inches vertically. Stagger the rows across the wall so the ties are no more than 24 inches apart. Fasten the ties with 8- or 10-penny ringshank nails or galvanized deck screws. Embed the ties completely in the mortar.

BUILDING CORNER LEADS

When building a corner lead, you need to lay bricks going in two directions in an alternating pattern so the bricks will lock together. Keep this simple rule in mind: The number of bricks you lay in the first course should equal the number of courses in your lead. For example, if you want your lead to be nine courses high, lay five bricks in one direction and four bricks in the other. That will give you a base for a lead with nine courses.

CAUTION

CHECK FAST

Check alignment immediately after laying the first few bricks. If you wait too long, the bricks will absorb too much of the mortar's moisture; you won't be able to move the bricks without causing the mortar to crumble.

Laying single-tier brick veneer *(continued)*

8 STRIKE THE JOINTS.

Using the concave jointer needed to produce the mortar joint of your choice (see page 147), strike the head (vertical) joints first, then the bed (horizontal) joints. Strike the joints soon after laying the bricks. If you wait too long, the mortar will stiffen and be unworkable.

9 CLEAN WITH A BRUSH.

After striking the joints, let the mortar set up for a while, then remove the burrs and crumbs of mortar left along the joints. Use a stiff brush for smaller pieces and a trowel for larger ones. Clean off mortar smears with a dampened rag and a brush, taking care not to soak any mortar joints.

10 INSTALL ROW-LOCK HEADER BRICKS.

To brick up the bottom of a windowsill or to cap off a veneer that extends only partway up a wall, set row-lock headers, as shown here, or headers that are laid flat. Install flashing and weep holes (see page 101). You may have to cut the bricks or adjust the joints to make the headers fit.

11 INSTALL ANGLE-IRON HEADERS.

To support bricks that go over doorways and windows, secure a $3\frac{1}{2} \times 3\frac{1}{2} \times \frac{1}{4}$-inch angle-iron header across the opening. Ends should rest on the course, even with the top of the opening. At least 4 inches of the angle should rest on the brick walls at both ends.

12 COVER TOP GAPS WITH MOLDING.

If you brick all the way up to a soffit, cover the gap between the soffit and the top course of brick with molding. This gives the job a finished look and keeps out moisture and insects. Nailing can be tricky. Angle galvanized finishing nails into the framing behind the fascia or straight up into the fascia itself. Caulk the seam between the molding and the brick.

EXPANSION JOINTS

Wherever a new masonry wall butts up against an existing wood, brick, or concrete surface, avoid bonding the two together firmly. Over the years, settling and expansion and contraction resulting from weather changes cause the two surfaces to move in different directions. Seal the joint between them with a material that is flexible. Expansion joint material is made for this purpose. Secure it to the existing wall before you begin work, and butt your new wall against it. Or after the new wall is built, cram oakum (a plumbing material) into the gap. Finish with a thick bead of high-quality silicone, acrylic with silicone, or butyl caulk.

BUILDING A GARDEN WALL

In addition to being an attractive landscape feature, a plain garden wall is an ideal way to learn bricklaying, particularly if you are planning a more ambitious project and want to hone your skills. For more about the techniques used, see pages 86–88. See page 98 for pattern options.

YOU'LL NEED

TIME: One day for a footing; a full day to lay bricks for a 16-foot-long, 3-foot-high wall.

SKILLS: Excavating, building forms, laying and finishing concrete, beginner skills in laying brick.

TOOLS: Concrete tools, wheelbarrow, pointed trowel, mason's hoe, stiff brush, mason's line, line blocks.

1 SET THE FOOTING AND LAY BRICKS.

Dig a footing that is 2 inches longer than the wall, twice the width of the wall, and as deep as the frost line in your area. Form the edge of the footing with 2×4s (see pages 35–36) or let your hole act as the form. Pour concrete to just below grade. Allow the concrete to cure for several days.

Snap chalk lines along the footing to define the perimeter of the wall, which should be centered on the footing. Lay the bricks using the same techniques as for a veneer wall (see pages 100–102), checking for plumb, level, and alignment as you work.

As you set the bricks in two rows together, embed corrugated metal brick ties in the mortar about every 12 inches in every third or fourth course.

2 TOP OFF THE WALL WITH HEADERS.

Once the wall reaches the desired height, cap it with headers. You can use formed concrete headers, header bricks laid flat, row-lock headers (as shown), flagstones, or limestone block. Slope the headers slightly to allow for drainage.

DRAINAGE FOR A RETAINING WALL

If your wall is freestanding, there is no need to worry about drainage, other than sloping the headers slightly. But if your wall is more than 2 feet high and is cut into a slope or holds back a terraced planting area, it will have to bear substantial water pressure when the ground becomes wet. In such a case, be sure to provide drainage in the form of a sloped perforated drainpipe set in a bed of gravel (see pages 83–84).

INSTALLING LIGHTWEIGHT BRICK VENEER

It's seldom possible to install a single-tier brick wall on an interior wall; floors simply will not support the weight. Even a basement floor can't bear the weight; footings undergird only the foundation walls, not the slab.

However, lightweight veneers can be applied to interior walls, and they look nearly as attractive as real brick. Because they are fire-retardant, you can use them for fire walls behind wood-burning stoves (see pages 118–119).

YOU'LL NEED

TIME: A day for an 8×10-foot wall.

SKILLS: Applying adhesive, measuring, leveling, cutting.

TOOLS: Trowel recommended by manufacturer, hammer, mason's line, line level, hacksaw with masonry blade, brush, jointer.

1 APPLY THE ADHESIVE.

Start in an upper corner of a wall. Spread a ⅛-inch layer of mortar adhesive over a 2×4-foot area.

For outside walls use roofing nails to nail a moisture barrier of 15-pound roofer's felt and a layer of metal lath to the walls. Then trowel on a coat of mortar, working in 2×3-foot sections.

2 INSTALL THE BRICKS.

Start at the top of the wall to ensure there will be a full course of brick where appearance counts. Attach a string running the length of the wall, held out from the wall about ½ inch, exactly one course down from the ceiling. Use a line level to make sure the string is level. If your ceiling is wavy or out of level, you may need to bring the line down a bit to make room for every brick. Press each brick into the adhesive, twisting it slightly to ensure a good bond. Align the bricks to the string. Leave ⅜ inch between bricks for normal-looking joints. To cut bricks use a hacksaw with a masonry cutting blade or rod.

3 STRIKE THE JOINTS.

Fill the joints between the bricks with more mortar adhesive or use a colored mortar after the adhesive has dried. Use either a pencil-type brush or a grout bag with the correct tip. Avoid smearing mortar adhesive on the face of the bricks; wipe up spills immediately. Once the joints have dried, coat the wall with a sealer recommended by the dealer.

MEASUREMENTS

To determine if you must start with a full or a partial brick, divide the length of each brick, plus the width of the mortar joint, into the width of your wall. This will tell you how many full bricks you'll need for each course. If the answer contains a remainder, you'll need to start with a partial brick.

The length of the first and last bricks should be the same, so divide any fraction of a brick by two to determine how long the starting brick should be. Avoid narrow fragments of brick. If the remainder is less than 4 inches, divide the remainder in half and trim that amount from the first and last brick in each course.

INSTALLING STONE VENEER

Lightweight stone veneers may be made of manufactured stone or cast from concrete and given natural-looking colors and textures. Stone veneer pieces range from ½–2 inches in thickness. With some lighter products, you can use an adhesive to attach the pieces directly on a finished interior wall (see page 104). With heavier material you'll need to apply expanded metal lath and attach the pieces with mortar.

YOU'LL NEED

TIME: Two days to cover an 8×10-foot wall.

SKILLS: Arranging stone in a pleasing pattern, cutting stone, applying metal lath and mortar.

TOOLS: Hammer, tin snips, flat finishing trowel, plasterer's rake or a homemade scratcher (see page 107), brick set, jointer, brush.

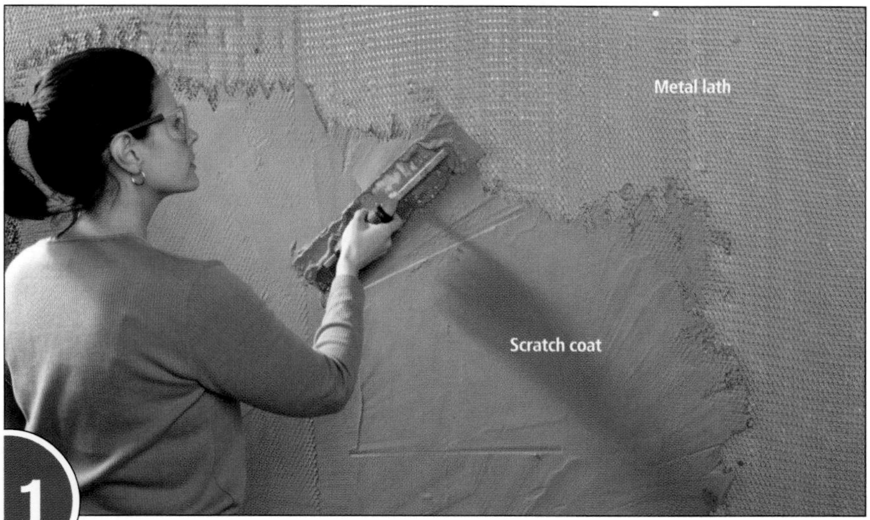

1 APPLY LATH AND FIRST MORTAR COAT.

For interior walls, fasten expanded metal lath onto the wall surface, nailing into studs. For exterior walls, nail on 15-pound roofing felt, then metal lath. Trowel on a ¼-inch coat of mortar over the lath. After the mortar has just begun to set up, roughen the surface with a plasterer's rake, scratching it to a depth of ⅛ inch. Let this coat dry and cure for 48 hours before applying the next layer of mortar and the stone. Meanwhile lay the stones out on the floor as they will be positioned on the wall. As you arrange them, keep the joint spaces consistent.

2 APPLY STONE VENEER.

Cover the scratch coat of mortar with a ½-inch layer of mortar, working with an 8-square-foot area at a time. Just before positioning each stone, also apply a thin layer of mortar to the back of the stone veneer. Press the stone into the mortar bed, moving it back and forth and rocking it slightly to create a thorough bond. Place the bottom corner stones first. Then, working upward, add pieces toward the center of the area you are veneering, keeping the joint space you established in your plan. (See page 67 for instructions for cutting stone.)

3 STRIKE THE JOINTS.

As soon as the mortar has stiffened but before it has set, use a jointer to strike the joints. Brush away the crumbs and burrs at the joint edges. Immediately clean any mortar off the face of stones with a damp rag and brush. Avoid soaking the mortar joints.

APPLYING STUCCO

Stucco makes an excellent exterior surface. It is durable and weather-resistant, has a pleasing texture, and can be painted. Even in severe climates, you'll find older houses with stucco still in mint condition.

A stucco finish is nothing more than two or three thin coats of a mortar that is 1 part masonry cement to 3 parts sand, with a small amount of lime and water added. Stucco requires a solid backing. Never apply it over fiberboard sheathing or foam insulation. Both of these materials give enough that a well-thrown baseball can dent or puncture the stucco wall.

If left untinted, stucco dries to a medium gray color. You can add an oxide pigment to the finish coat or stain or paint the surface after the top coat has cured. If you mix in pigment, carefully measure and mix each batch exactly the same way to obtain a consistent color. You can make a bright white stucco by mixing together white portland cement, lime, and white silica sand for the finish coat.

There are many possibilities for the final texture. The examples shown above right represent some of the standard options. But you can experiment with different trowels and techniques to find the texture that pleases you. Just make sure you can reproduce the texture consistently over a broad area.

YOU'LL NEED

TIME: A day for preparation and each coat on an 8×20-foot wall.

SKILLS: Troweling with smooth, even strokes.

TOOLS: Brush, hammer, tin snips, flat trowel, hock, plasterer's rake or homemade scratcher, hose. (For scratched finish texture, a brush or whisk broom.)

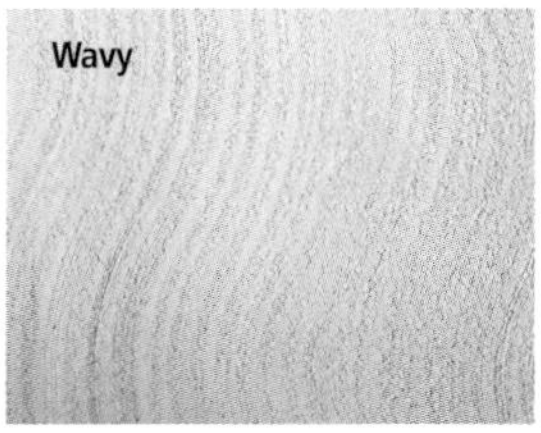

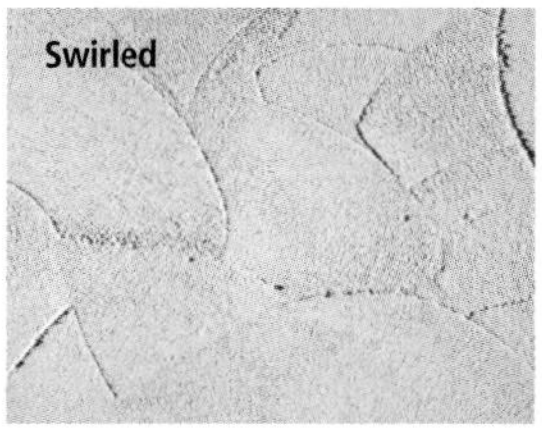

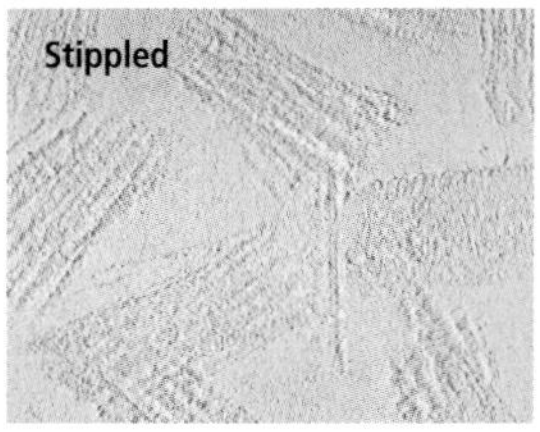

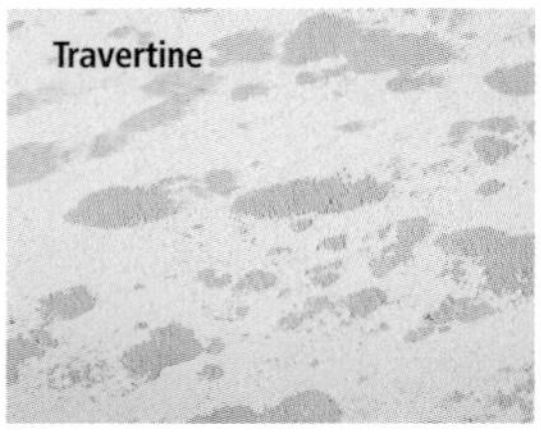

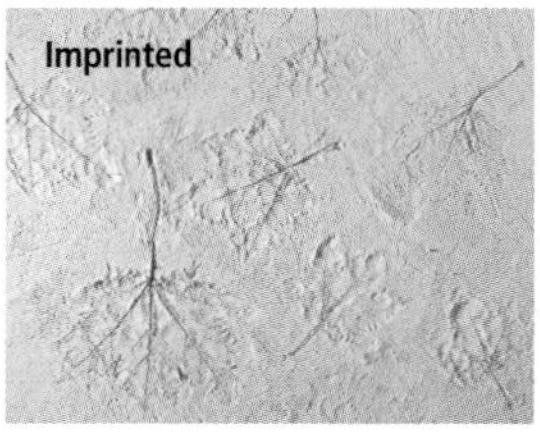

To achieve a smooth, plasterlike appearance, trowel the final coat several times as it becomes progressively stiffer. For a swirled texture, trowel the mortar just once, using an arcing motion, and allow the resulting pattern to remain. For a wavy, scratched surface, trowel the mortar smooth, allow it to harden slightly, then draw a brush across it lightly. The stiffer the brush, the coarser the pattern.

To stipple the top coat, hold a whisk broom at an angle to the wall and pat the surface with the ends of the bristles in an irregular pattern. For a travertine finish, spatter on a coat of thin mortar in a contrasting color and trowel it slightly after it has stiffened. You can use leaves or other items to make imprints in the soft mortar; then lightly trowel the surface.

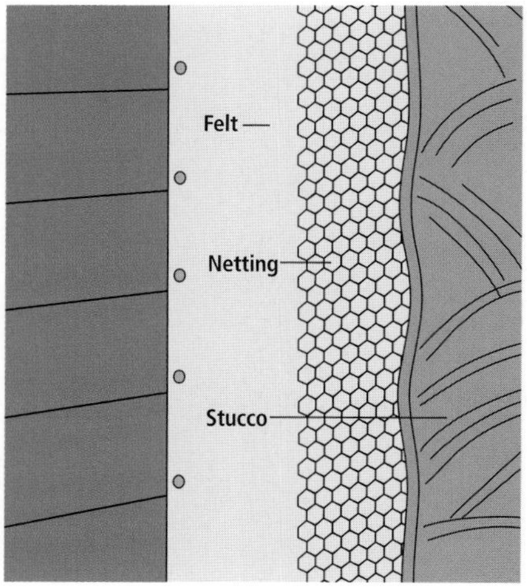

1 PREPARE WALL AND APPLY FIRST COAT.

For a concrete, brick, or block wall, first brush on concrete bonding agent and allow it to dry. Apply stucco directly to the wall.

To apply stucco over a wood-frame wall, staple 15-pound roofing felt to the sheathing, then cover it with 17-gauge metal netting (buy 150-foot rolls to minimize seams). Cut the netting with tin snips and attach it with galvanized roofing nails.

Apply the scratch coat with a flat finishing trowel. Trowel on a ¼- to ½-inch layer of mortar, forcing it into the netting so some extrudes through the netting to "key" the coating in place.

2

SCRATCH THE FIRST COAT.

Once you begin a wall, always complete it to avoid start-and-stop lines. Allow the scratch coat to harden only slightly, then scratch it with a plasterer's rake or a homemade tool such as the one shown. (To make the tool, drive 4-penny galvanized nails through a piece of 2×2 at 1-inch intervals.) Scratch the entire mortar surface to a depth of about 1/8 inch, running the tool in long lines along the surface.

3

KEEP THE MORTAR WET.

As with all concrete or mortar products, slow, damp curing provides the greatest strength. Allow the scratch coat to cure for 36–48 hours; keep it damp by periodically misting it with water from a garden hose. Watch the weather; you'll need to mist more often on a hot, dry day than on a cool, damp day. Avoid wet-dry cycles; they create cracks.

4

APPLY THE FINISH COAT.

With a flat finishing trowel, apply a 1/8- to 1/4-inch-thick finish coat onto the dampened scratch or brown coat (see box at right). If you add powdered pigment, add water to the pigment and mix it completely before adding it to the stucco. Finish to the texture of your choice (see page 106). Allow the stucco to cure for several days, misting the surface occasionally to slow the curing process. Complete the project by caulking around doors and windows. Wait at least six weeks before you paint the stucco, and use a paint formulated to cover concrete.

THE BROWN COAT

For an extra-strong stucco wall, you can apply a coat of mortar between the scratch and the finish coats. This is called the brown coat.

Apply the brown coat soon after you scratch the scratch coat. If you must wait before applying the brown coat, keep the scratch coat wet after scratching it to prevent curing. Mix, apply, and scratch the brown coat in the same way as you did the scratch coat. Allow it to set for a few hours and keep it moist for two days for a slow cure.

INSTALLING POLYMER STUCCO

The stucco technique on pages 106–107 is the least expensive way to cover a wall with stucco, but it takes a long time. It can be especially tedious to keep the various coats moist for several days. New products and techniques are now available. The materials are more expensive, but installation is easier.

Flashing and a water barrier are installed in such a way that water that comes into the wall (through small openings around windows, for example) can escape, keeping studs and insulation dry. Instead of a scratch coat of stucco, sheets of cement board form the substrate. This provides a straight, even surface, something not easy to achieve with standard stucco methods. The cement board is covered with a thin coat of portland cement, then with a coat of aggregated polymer, which is applied without special troweling techniques. Available in many colors, the polymer surface resists dirt and cleans more easily than a standard stucco finish.

YOU'LL NEED

TIME: A day to cover about 200 square feet.

SKILLS: Carpentry, smoothly applying polymer.

TOOLS: Hammer, chalk line, level, stapler, trowel, knife, drywall square.

CAUTION

BEWARE OF INSULATION-BASED SYSTEMS

Some polymer systems use sheets of soft insulating material, such as polystyrene, instead of cement board as the base for the polymer. Such systems have two serious problems: They trap moisture inside walls and dent easily.

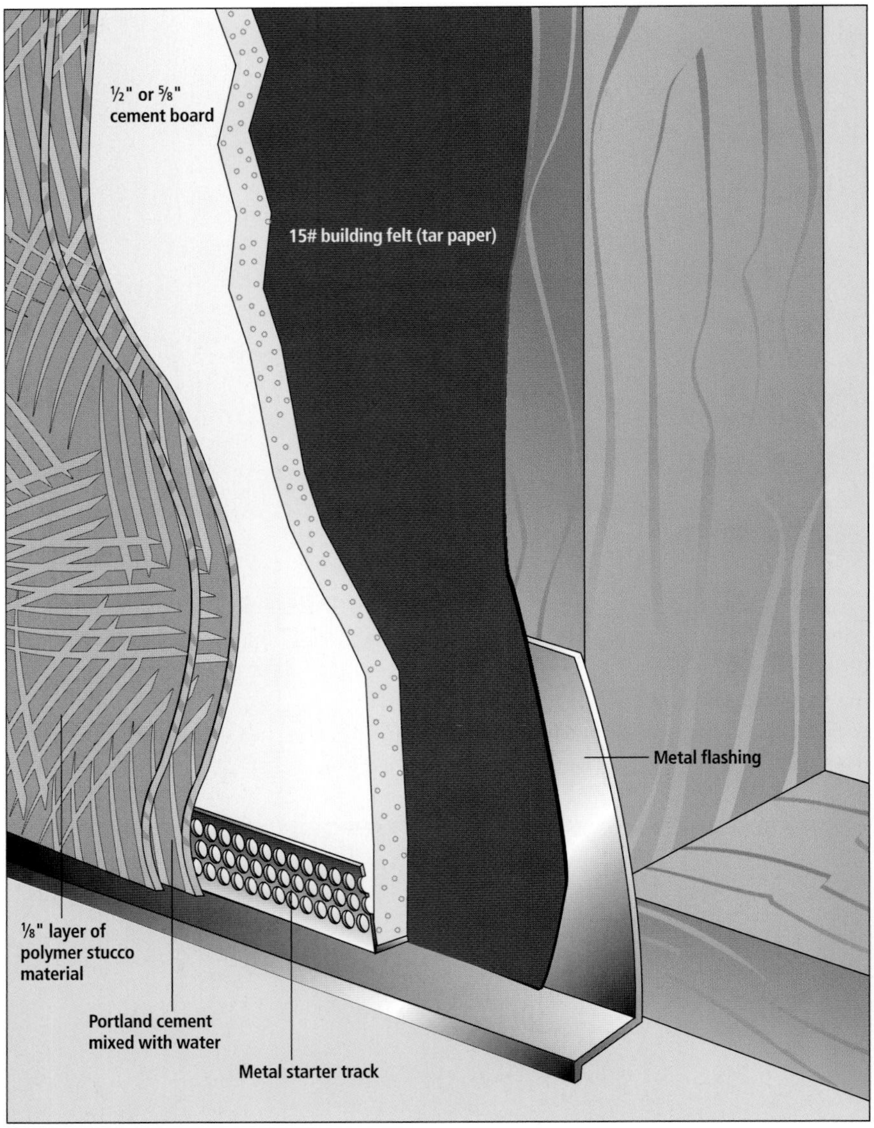

INSTALL A POLYMER STUCCO WALL.

Remove window and door moldings and trim out with filler blocks that are the same thickness as the new stucco wall (see page 106). Along the bottom of the wall, use a level and chalk line to mark a line, then install flashing along the line. Staple 15-pound building felt (tar paper) to the wall, taking care not to rip it. Overlap joints about 3 inches. Install a metal starter track on the flashing.

Attach the cement board sheets by slipping them into the starter track and fastening them with 2-inch roofing nails or screws designed for cement board. To cut cement board, use a drywall square and a utility knife. Cut into the board and through the mesh on one side, break back the board, and cut through the mesh on the other side. Fill in joints between cement boards with a mixture of portland cement and water.

Once that sets, cover the entire surface with a thin coat of the portland cement mixture. After that layer dries, trowel on the polymer texture to a thickness of about ⅛ inch.

INSTALLING GLASS BLOCKS

Glass block walls and windows allow filtered light to pass into your house while providing security and some insulation.

If you are using glass block to replace an existing window, remove the window and jamb so the glass block will be joined to a masonry surface or directly to the framing of your wall.

You'll save money by assembling the blocks yourself as shown at right. An easier but more expensive way to install glass block is to order a preassembled panel. Measure your opening carefully, making allowances for out-of-square openings. Then order a preassembled unit from an outlet that specializes in glass block. The ready-made unit consists of blocks already mortared together; the whole unit will be held together with a metal strap. It will be extremely heavy if the window is large. Lay a bed of mortar on the sill, set the entire unit in place, and fill in mortar all around it.

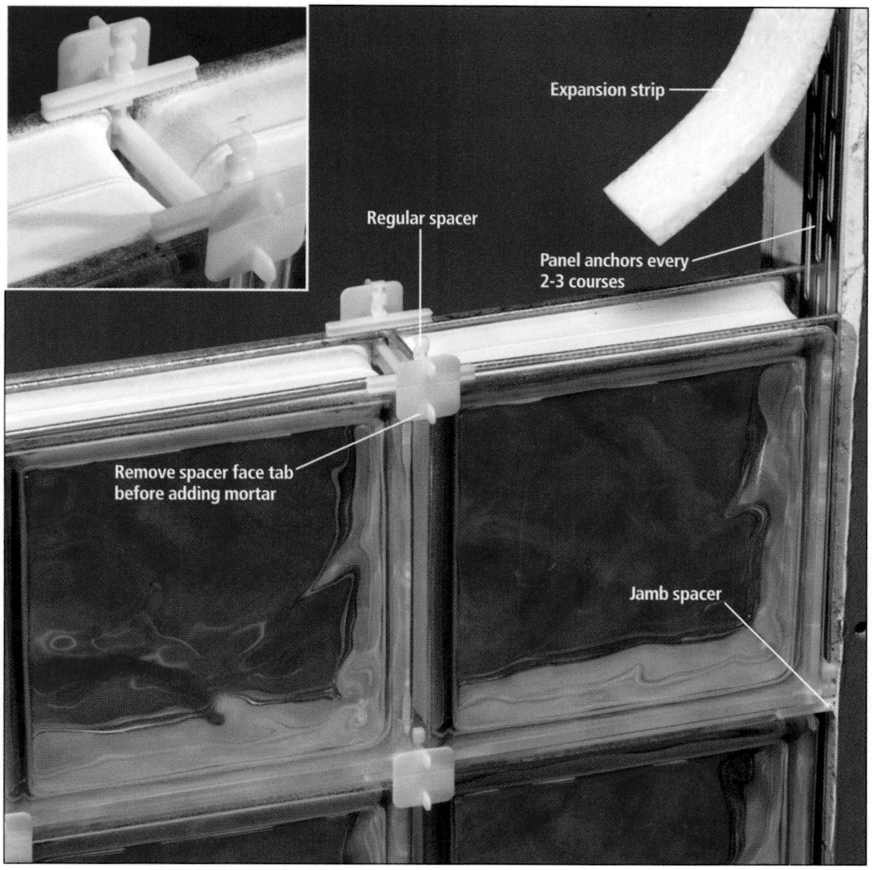

YOU'LL NEED

TIME: About one day to install blocks in a medium-size opening.

SKILLS: Careful measuring, laying masonry units in mortar.

TOOLS: Trowel, sled jointer or joint strike.

INSTALL INDIVIDUAL GLASS BLOCKS.

Measure the opening and choose a pleasing pattern of blocks; there are several sizes available. Dry-fit the blocks using panel anchors screwed to the side jambs every few courses and expansion strips over the anchors and along the header. (You can snap off parts of the spacers to make the various types shown.)

Disassemble your dry-fit. Lay a bed of mortar on the sill and begin laying blocks. Twist off the spacer face tabs as you set the blocks in position. Throw mortar on the top edge of each course and butter the blocks as you would for a brick wall (see page 98). Use spacers to maintain consistent joint lines.

About every third course, embed the panel anchors in mortar and press reinforcing wire into the mortar. Don't put mortar on top of the final course of blocks. Strike the joints (see page 102), wipe the blocks clean, and caulk along the sides and header.

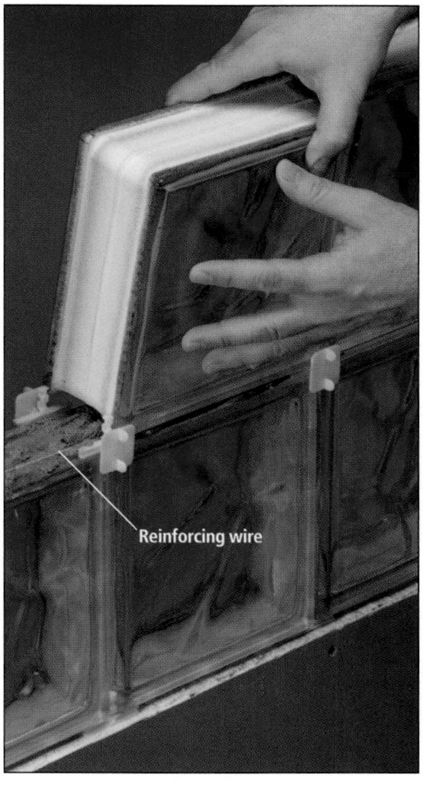

PROVIDE VENTILATION

Before you permanently glass-in an opening, consider ventilation requirements. If you want fresh air in the space you're closing up, install a vent or fan before installing the glass blocks, or install a vent module sized to replace two or more glass blocks.

Special PROJECTS

Whether you're looking for ideas for your first masonry project, or you want to add a unique, final touch to a long-standing project, use this chapter for inspiration.

A great beginner's masonry project that will add both beauty and utility to a front walkway or porch is a brick and cedar bench. A larger yet simple project is a stone and rail fence, which adds unassuming boundaries around your home. Spice up a garden with a curved-wall planter—its smooth lines are aesthetically pleasing, and the wall can act as a sitting space.

Experimenting with different types of stone and methods of laying them can make for one-of-a-kind paths and walkways. This chapter shows you how to install a path with pavers and a flagstone walkway. Timber and brick steps and a semicircular brick patio are two simple additions that will add visual interest to your home.

- Pages 114–115: Curved-wall planter.
- Page 116: Brick and cedar bench.
- Page 117: Stone and rail fence.
- Pages 118–119: Wood stove surround.
- Pages 120–121: Semicircular brick patio.
- Pages 122–123: Timber and brick steps.
- Page 124: Paver path.
- Page 125: Flagstone walkway.

PRETTY PATH
Instead of leaving grass between flagstones, as shown in the project on page 125, tuck flowers into the spaces of this infrequently traveled garden path.

A PLACE FOR PLANTS
The strong horizontal lines of this home are softened with the gentle curve of the wall planter. The brick shows off the colors of the garden plants while blending into the architecture of the home.

AN INTIMATE SETTING
A few chairs and a small table transforms this intimate garden setting into a place to relax or share good conversation with friends. By keeping the furniture simple and minimal, you can easily clear the area to make the space more functional.

EXPANSIVE POSSIBILITIES
This brick patio offers plenty of room for relaxing. Despite its size, creating a similar patio is within the capabilities of a do-it-yourselfer. This project is a variation of the semicircular patio featured on page 120. The bricks were installed over a slab, with a rectangular portion and a semicircular extension that gracefully curves into the yard.

<

PATCHWORK PATIO
Flagstone, dark green Scotch moss, and light green Irish moss blend to form a patchwork patio. Starting the moss requires regular watering; avoid using the patio until the root system becomes established.

>

SIMPLE STEPS
Gravel native to the area fills the timbers forming these steps, providing natural drainage. For a variation on this look, turn to page 122 to install timber-and-brick steps.

VISUAL INTEREST
Though planning and installing a curved patio such as this one requires a bit more work than a standard rectangular one, the result is visually pleasing and provides flexibility for incorporating existing landscape features such as mature trees.

FLAGSTONE PATH
This inviting flagstone walk is the perfect, understated companion to the lush garden on both sides. To install a similar flagstone pathway, turn to page 125.

BUILDING A CURVED-WALL PLANTER

A planter is a functional means for holding plants around your home, and by adding some flair to the structural design, you can notably change the shape of your yard.

If you have some experience laying straight brick walls, you'll be surprised how easy it is to build this graceful planter. The biggest challenge is laying out the plywood template; the bricklaying is easy.

As with other mortared brick walls, this project requires a footing. To avoid having your project ruined by frost heaving and cracking, check with your local building department about the frost line and footing depth required in your area.

GRACEFUL LINES.

The serpentine lines of this brick planter do more than lend it an elegant appearance. The curves actually add significant strength and vertical stability to the wall.

YOU'LL NEED

TIME: A day for the footing and a day for the brickwork.

SKILLS: Measuring and cutting curves, bricklaying.

TOOLS: Circular saw, hammer, pencil, string, saber saw, shovel, trowel, brick set, jointer.

1

CUT THE TEMPLATE.

From a full sheet of ½-inch plywood, cut 24×48-inch and 24×96-inch pieces. Fasten them together end to end with cleats and screws, as shown. Lay the plywood panel on a flat surface (a lawn or a driveway will do) and draw a straight baseline 2 inches from the long edge.

Measure from the baseline and the end of the sheet to locate the four radius centers shown (mark them on the lawn or driveway). Use a drywall square or a framing square to help you find the spots. From each radius center, draw two curved lines using a compass made out of a pencil and string. Have a helper hold the string at the radius center while you draw the lines. Draw all eight radii on the board. Use a saber saw to cut out the curves.

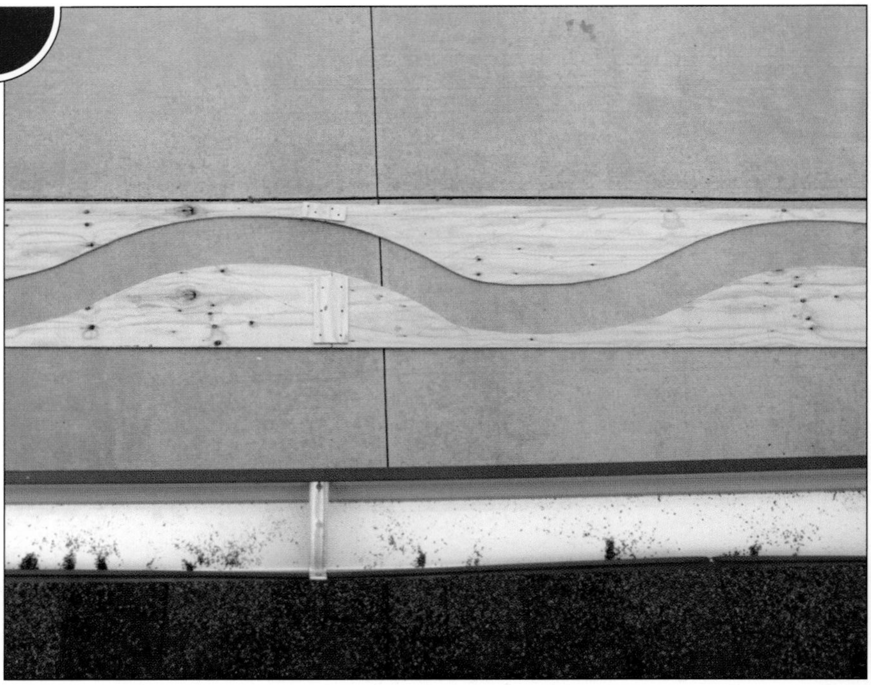

2 DIG AND POUR THE FOOTING.

Set the two template pieces on the ground at the wall site. Separate them so there is a consistent 8-inch gap between them (use lengthwise bricks as spacers). Drive in stakes and nail them to the template pieces to anchor the template firmly so it will not shift if you step on it while you dig.

With a square shovel, dig a trench for the footing. Dig several inches below the frost line or at least 12 inches deep if frost is not a problem in your area. Dig along the template and the straight areas of the wall. Tamp the soil and shovel in 2–3 inches of gravel. Pour concrete to within a couple inches of grade. Allow the footing to cure for a few days.

3 LAY THE BRICKS.

Use the template as a guide for laying the bricks. Make a one-course dry run to see how well full bricks fit and to adjust the width of vertical joints between them. Stagger the two tiers of bricks, as shown. (For more on building brick walls, see pages 99–102.) On the first course and every two courses thereafter, place metal ties across the tiers at 24-inch intervals. As you lay the course just above final grade, make weep holes (see page 101) every 12–18 inches. As you work, check the wall for plumb. Hold the outer template up against it every other course.

4 CAP THE WALL.

Top off the wall with row-lock headers. At the corners, position the bricks as shown in the lower portion of the drawing. Or for a more finished look, miter-cut the bricks using a circular saw with a masonry blade. Strike the joints and allow the mortar to cure for a few days. Coat the inside of the wall with a masonry waterproofing compound. In the planting area place 6 inches of sand or pea gravel for drainage. Cover with topsoil and add your plants.

BUILDING A BRICK AND CEDAR BENCH

The basic bench shown here combines two classic materials—brick and cedar—for rugged beauty and durability. Use a bench to dress up an entryway or create a resting spot in your yard.

The bench dimensions can be altered. Typically a seat should be 16–18 inches above the ground. Make the bench at least 16–24 inches deep and no more than 8 feet wide.

Use wood that resists splintering and is weather-resistant. The heartwood of cedar or redwood is the best choice because it is stable and unlikely to crack. You can tell heartwood by its darker color; cream-colored sapwood will not resist rot as well. Avoid using pressure-treated lumber for this project; it cracks easily and is not as attractive as redwood or cedar. You can stain the wood or leave it unfinished and allow it to turn a silvery gray.

YOU'LL NEED

TIME: 2 to 3 days, allowing time for concrete and mortar to cure.

SKILLS: Bricklaying, cutting and fastening lumber.

TOOLS: Mortar hoe, mortar box, brick trowel, pointing trowel, hammer, circular saw or handsaw, drill with wood bit and masonry bit, ratchet wrench.

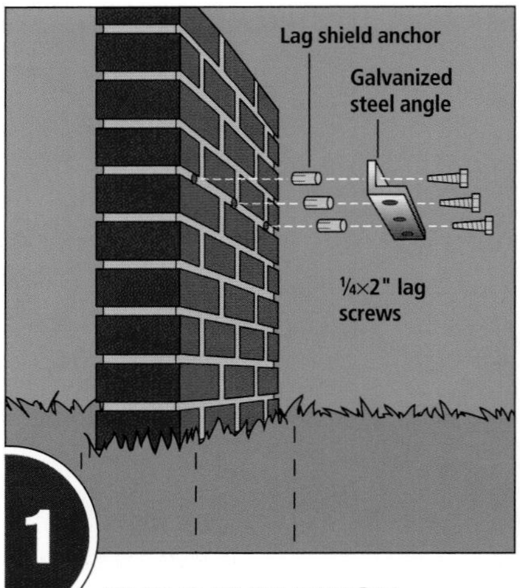

1 BUILD THE BRICK SUPPORTS.

Excavate and install footings (see pages 35–36). Allow the concrete to set for a day. Lay the brick support walls to a height two to four courses above the seat level (see pages 88–89, 98, and 103). Allow the mortar to cure for a few days. Then install steel angle irons, using lag bolts and shields. Drill the holes with a masonry bit.

2 ASSEMBLE THE SEAT.

Cut cedar 2×4s to fit between the brick supports. Cut 1×4 spacers 2 inches long. Place a set of spacers at each end of the seat and midway between. Nail the 2×4s and spacers together with 12-penny galvanized nails or 3-inch deck screws. Drill pilot holes for all the nails or screws to prevent the wood from splitting.

3 ATTACH THE SEAT.

Bore pilot holes in the seat and fasten it to the steel angle irons with ¼×2-inch lag screws. Be sure the screws go into the center of the 2×4s, not between the 2×4s and the spacers, or they will not hold well.

BUILDING A STONE-AND-RAIL FENCE

This fence firmly establishes a boundary yet leaves the view unrestricted. Because the rails are not joined permanently to the stone posts, replacing them is easy. For the posts, the rectangular shape of ashlar is easier to work with than irregular rubble.

Check building codes to make sure you place the fence correctly in relation to your property line and for electrical requirements. Carefully plot the location of the stone posts. If you will be using 8-foot-long poles, you'll want the facing walls of the posts to be no more than 7½ feet apart to provide support for the rails.

Begin by laying out and digging footings and the trench for the electric cable that powers the lamp. Stake the corners of the fence; using a mason's line stretched between the corner stakes, check for square using the 3-4-5 method (see page 25). Stake the corners of each post.

Dig footing holes below the frost line or at least 32 inches deep. Dig them as you would for a column footing (see page 39), but make them as large as the stone bases will be. For posts with no lamp, pour footings to within an inch of grade. See pages 138–139 for figuring concrete needs.

YOU'LL NEED

TIME: Several days for a fence with 6 or 7 posts.

SKILLS: Laying stone.

TOOLS: Shovel, level, hammer, mason's trowel, pointing trowel.

CAUTION

Check building codes to see if you can run waterproof, underground-feed (UF) cable in the ground or if you need to protect cable with rigid conduit. Also find out how deep the cable needs to be. Locate utilities before digging.

1 INSTALL A LAMPPOST.

Use the footing hole for the lamppost also. Dig the footing hole and a trench for the electric cable (check local codes). Run the cable to the post, making sure the cable entry hole is above the level of the concrete footing. Stabilize the post with bracing and pour in the concrete.

2 BUILD THE POSTS.

Build the ashlar stone posts using the techniques on pages 88–89. Make the posts 42–48 inches tall. Leave the inside of the posts hollow. Insert rails loosely into the openings as you lay the stones, making sure rails are parallel to the ground. Use large stone pieces to cap off posts.

INSTALLING A WOOD STOVE SURROUND

A wood-burning stove radiates heat in all directions, so you must place it on a noncombustible surface and maintain safe clearances from walls and other combustible surfaces. Follow local building codes and the manufacturer's recommendations to determine the best location for a stove and the correct size of the hearth and fire wall.

Run the flue pipe before installing the veneer. Use brick veneer on the wall. For the hearth you can use brick veneer, as shown here, or full-size bricks.

YOU'LL NEED

TIME: About one day to install the brick once the walls, chimney flue, and floor are prepared.

SKILLS: Laying out and installing brick veneer.

TOOLS: Hammer, tape measure, modular spacing rule, carpenter's level, notched trowel, brick set, small sledgehammer.

CAUTION

SAFE INSTALLATION AND USE OF A WOOD-BURNING STOVE

Modern wood-burning stoves are highly efficient, burning logs completely and sending little heat up the chimney. Follow the manufacturer's installation instructions carefully. Use only a masonry chimney or a metal, Class-A-rated chimney. Be sure the chimney is high enough above the roofline to draw well. Clean the flue regularly; as wood burns, it produces creosote, which accumulates in the flue, creating a fire hazard.

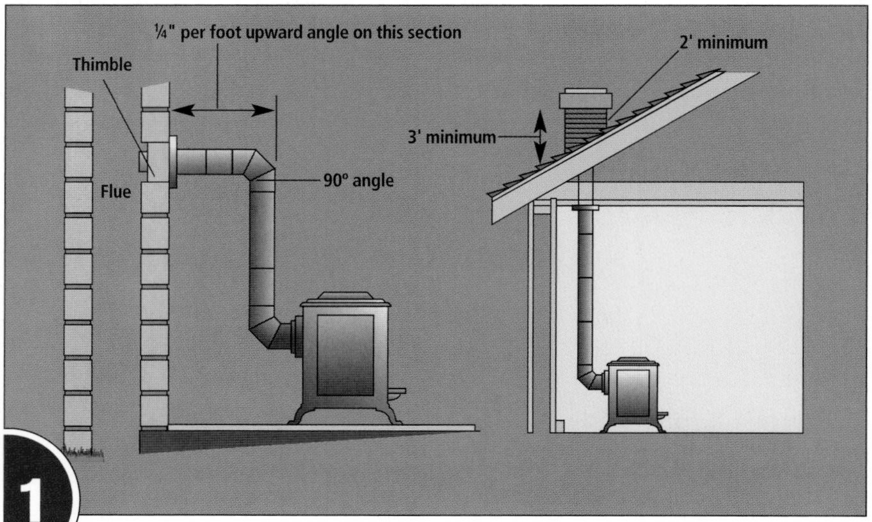

1 PLAN THE LOCATION.

Shown above are two options for venting a wood-burning stove. You can install a masonry flue in the wall or extend a Class-A metal flue up through the roof. Before you begin the project, check local requirements for chimney height above the roofline. Assemble the chimney and flue so you know exactly where the stove needs to be located. As you assemble the metal chimney, fit the sections together with the crimped ends pointing toward the stove. That way any condensing moisture will flow back to the fire and dissipate.

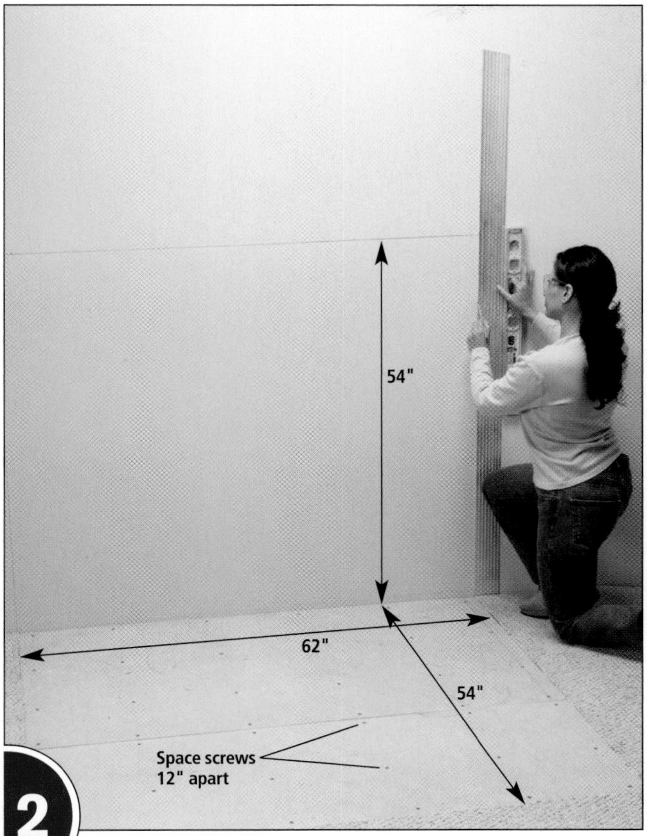

LAY OUT THE JOB.

Based on the manufacturer's recommendations and local codes, decide on the dimensions of your hearth and fire wall. To avoid cutting too many bricks, use a modular spacing rule (see page 128) to set your dimensions.

Use a level and straightedge to mark the outline of the fire wall on the existing wall. Lay out the radius corners on the hearth using a string-and-pencil compass. The corners shown are 16-inch radii; you can vary the shape of the corner according to the shape of your stove and how much hearth area you want in front of it.

If you have carpeting, cut out the carpet and its pad. Remove a section of baseboard molding wide enough to accommodate the fire wall. If required by code, first screw ¼-inch-thick cement board to the floor and wall. Screws on the wall should attach to studs.

LAY THE BRICKS.

Depending on the composition of the brick veneer material, you may be able to apply thinset mortar to the wall and attach the veneer directly to it. If not see page 105 for applying a scratch coat and mortar. Use shallow plastic spacers to maintain consistent joints between the bricks. When applying the brick veneer to the wall, check for level and plumb with a carpenter's level.

Dry-fit the bricks for the hearth border to establish joint spacing before laying them permanently in mortar. Then start in a corner and lay the remainder of the floor bricks. Cut the bricks with a brick set and small sledgehammer. Wait a day for the bricks to set, then grout the joints (see page 104).

INSTALLING A SEMICIRCULAR BRICK PATIO

A semicircular patio looks complicated, but installing it requires little more skill than a rectangular patio. In fact only the central core requires cut bricks, so you may need to cut fewer bricks than for other designs.

As with all masonry work, have the bricks or pavers delivered close to the site to minimize lifting and hauling.

YOU'LL NEED

TIME: About two days to install a 200-square-foot patio.

SKILLS: Ability to lay out a semicircular pattern, cutting brick.

TOOLS: Round-point shovel, rake, tamper, mason's line, rebar, carpenter's level, hammer, screed, brick set, baby sledgehammer, broom, hose.

OTHER OPTIONS FOR CURVED EDGINGS

This project uses ¼-inch hardboard as a temporary edging for the patio. For a permanent edging you may be able to find redwood bender board, which is about ¼ inch thick and 3½ inches wide. Or ask your lumberyard to rip clear 1×4 redwood along its thickness, leaving you with two pieces about 5⁄16 inch thick. If you soak the redwood in water for a couple of hours, it will bend easily without cracking. Other permanent edgings include steel ribbon, plastic, and bricks set in concrete (see page 61).

1 INSTALL THE EDGING.

To create the semicircle, drive a stake at the center of the space and tie a piece of rebar with a mason's line at the desired radius. Pull the line taut, keeping the rebar vertical, to mark the locations of stakes evenly spaced about every about 2 feet. Excavate to a 4-inch depth.

Set the hardboard edging in place, bending and leveling it as you go. Attach it to the stakes with screws so it is 1 inch above grade. Check for a smooth curve. Stakes are difficult to install accurately; you may need to unscrew the edging at some points and use shims to correct the curve.

2 SCREED THE SITE.

Tamp the soil and cover the site with landscaping fabric. Fill the area with crushed gravel and sand, or sand alone, until it is 1–2 inches below the edging. Rake it as smooth and level as you can.

Notch one end of a straight 2×4 screed so that it rides along the edging as you smooth the base. The depth of the notch should equal the thickness of the bricks or pavers. Install a 2×4 pivot base for the screed, taking care to stake it so the top edge of the screed will be level. Screed the sand, tamp it down with a hand or power vibrating tamper, then screed again.

Refer to pages 62–65 for detailed instructions on laying a patio surface.

3 INSTALL THE BRICKS OR PAVERS.

Start at the outside of the form and lay all the border bricks. Then work inward, completing each course before moving on to the next. Once you've laid several courses, avoid kneeling or standing directly on the bricks. Use pieces of plywood on the bricks as kneelers.

Every few courses check your work by scribing an arc with the string compass. The joints between the bricks or pavers will be slightly wedge-shaped and larger at the end nearest the edging. After the bricks are laid, sweep extra-fine sand into the joints, moisten with a fine spray, and sweep in more sand where needed. Remove the hardboard edging and fill soil firmly around the perimeter.

MAKE THE BASE FIRM

Take extra care when installing and tamping down the subsurface of your patio. The curved edge of a patio like this one is especially prone to sinking and buckling over the years because it is not held firmly in place. Even the permanent edgings described on page 120 are not extremely strong.

You may want to dig a little deeper near the perimeter and install some gravel as well as sand. If you use a hand tamper, do a thorough job; take turns with a helper. The best way to ensure a solid subsurface is to rent a power vibrating tamper.

INSTALLING TIMBER-AND-BRICK STEPS

Steps like these take about the same time to build as concrete steps (see pages 32–34). The result, however, is more stylish and inviting. If the timbers are fastened firmly with rebar and spikes, and the sand bed is well tamped, the steps will be nearly as solid as concrete and much easier to repair.

Choose timbers that will withstand the climate in your region. Pressure-treated landscaping timbers are readily available; choose from 5×6s, 6×6s, and 6×8s. Pave the steps with severe weathering (SW) brick (see page 130).

YOU'LL NEED

TIME: About one day to build a landing with two or three steps.

SKILLS: Laying out stairs, cutting timbers, laying brick.

TOOLS: Small sledgehammer, brick set, circular saw, tamper, mason's line, line or carpenter's level, tape measure, story pole or modular spacing rule, drill with long bit or bit extension, rubber mallet, broom, hose.

STAIR HEIGHT AND DEPTH

Because an entry stairway is used often, it should be comfortable for walking. Laying 6×8 timbers narrow side up creates 7½-inch step rises, a comfortable height for most people. For elderly people or children, 6×6 timbers will make a shallower step. A suitable depth for a single step is 11–12 inches. Add 1-foot increments for deeper steps.

TIMBER AND BRICK INLAY.

A timber and brick inlay can be suitable for an informal or formal entryway to your home, deck, or patio. Consider using older bricks for a more rustic look, or laying the bricks in a more sophisticated pattern for a formal design.

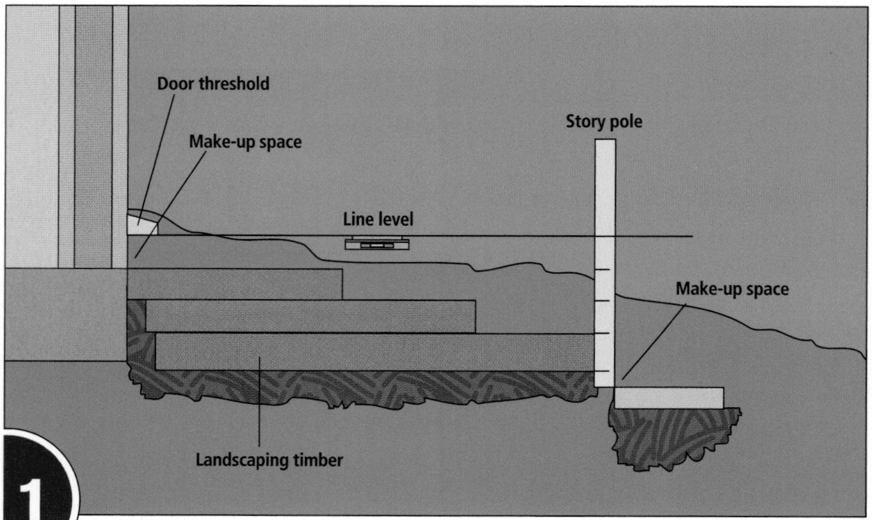

1 LAY OUT THE STAIRS.

The rise of each step is determined by the thickness of the timber you use. If the total rise is not evenly divisible by that thickness, make up the difference at the lowest step and the door sill. Avoid making the bottom step more than 1 inch higher than the rest. (See page 32 to figure rise and run for a stairway.) Use a line level and a homemade story pole (or modular spacing rule) to determine your layout. For a short stairway use a straight 2×4 and carpenter's level instead of the line level.

2 BUILD THE FRAME.

Excavate the site according to your plan layout. But when you dig, allow an extra 6 inches of working space on each side. Lay a 2-inch bed of well-tamped gravel for the bottom timbers. Make sure the steps slope away from the house $\frac{1}{4}$ inch per running foot. Where the tops of the timbers will not show, drill $\frac{3}{8}$-inch holes about every 2 feet and drive 3-foot pieces of rebar through the timbers and into the ground to anchor the steps. Where the tops will show, drill long pilot holes with a $\frac{3}{16}$-inch bit and fasten the timbers together with 12-inch spikes.

WORKING WITH TIMBERS

You will need high-quality, long-shank $\frac{3}{8}$- and $\frac{3}{16}$-inch drill bits to bore holes through the landscaping timbers for the spikes and rebar. A normal-length bit attached to a bit extension also will work but tends to come loose with use.

Drilling through the timbers will put a strain on 3.0- or 3.2-amp drills. Don't force the bit; allow the drill to cool frequently. You can rent or buy a more powerful drill that will handle the job with ease.

Cut the timbers by sawing all four sides with a circular saw, then sawing the middle with a handsaw. This method takes some time, so if you have a lot of cutting to do, rent an oversize circular saw.

3 SCREED AND TAMP.

Starting with the bottom step, tamp the gravel firm, then spread 2 to 3 inches of sand. Notch a screed board the thickness of the bricks or pavers and screed the sand to that level. Tamp, add more sand if needed, then screed again. Once you install the bricks, move to the next step up and prepare it in the same way. (See pages 62–65 for more on laying bricks in sand.)

4 LAY THE BRICKS OR PAVERS.

Choose a pattern (see page 60) and install the step surface. Cut the pavers or bricks with a brick set and small sledgehammer or use a masonry saw or a circular saw with a masonry blade. Use a rubber mallet to pound in hard-to-fit bricks. Once each section is finished, spread fine sand on the surface and sweep it into the joints. Gently spray with water, add more sand, and repeat the process until the joints are filled.

INSTALLING A PAVER PATH

If possible place paths made of pavers several feet away from trees and bushes. Otherwise their roots could buckle the surface of the path. Read pages 62–65 for information on laying patio surfaces in sand.

Determine the width of your path by dry-laying a row of pavers. Choose a layout that will avoid having to cut a lot of pavers or use small pieces.

It is important that the edging pieces be installed firmly in place; on a narrow path there will be considerable pressure exerted on them. If the soil is loose, use extra-long stakes to hold the edging in place. After the path is built, drive in extra stakes if the edging appears to be moving outward or if the joints between the pavers are getting wider.

YOU'LL NEED

TIME: About two days to excavate and install a 3-foot-wide by 15-foot-long path.

SKILLS: Excavating, leveling, laying masonry units in sand.

TOOLS: Small sledgehammer, brick set, tamper, framing square, level, rented masonry saw.

EXCAVATE, INSTALL EDGING, SCREED, TAMP, AND LAY PAVERS.

Lay out the path and excavate at least 6 inches deep and 6 inches wider than the path, including the edging. Remove all organic material. Lay and tamp a 1½-inch bed of gravel and install 2×4 edging, checking it for level and staking it at least every 4 feet. Use heartwood of redwood or cedar, or pressure-treated lumber.

Lay landscaping fabric between the edging and shovel in sand. Make a screed from a 2×6, notching it to a depth equal to the thickness of your pavers. For drainage you may want to crown the path by making a curved screed (see page 64). Screed and tamp the sand firmly.

Set the pavers in place. You can use a brick set and small sledgehammer to cut the pavers, but because the cut edges will be so visible, you may want to rent a masonry cutoff saw. Use a framing square to true up the courses every few feet. When all the pavers are laid, spread fine sand and sweep it into the joints. Spray it with water and sweep in more sand as needed.

INSTALLING A FLAGSTONE WALKWAY

For a casual walkway that looks as if it has been in place for years, consider a flagstone path. You can achieve a seasoned look by leaving sod between the stones. As with any masonry material set directly into the soil, these stones will settle with time and will have to be reset every few years.

Begin by laying out the path. Lay a charged hose (close the nozzle and turn on the water) on the ground in the pattern you want. Pour flour or sand over it to establish the path's outlines. (See pages 66–67 for more about laying flagstones in soil.)

YOU'LL NEED

TIME: Several hours to install about 50 square feet of flagstone.

SKILLS: No special skills needed.

TOOLS: Hose, shovel, garden trowel, small sledgehammer, brick set.

1 LAY OUT THE FLAGSTONES.

Following the outline for your path, lay the stones directly on the ground. Turn them in different directions and try different stones until you come up with a pattern with fairly consistent joint lines that are about 1½ inches wide. Combine large and small stones as you lay out the pattern. If you need to cut a stone, use a small sledgehammer and brick set to etch a ⅛-inch-deep line on both sides of the stone. Support the stone along the cut line and strike the waste side until it breaks (see page 67). Slice the sod around the first stone.

2 EXCAVATE AND TAMP.

Move a stone away. Dig out the sod, being careful to preserve the sod between the stones. Remove roots or stones that might make it difficult to set the stone level. Fill the hole with soil or sand as necessary and tamp it firmly.

3 PLACE THE STONE.

If a stone rocks or wobbles when you step on it, take it out and note the pattern of indentations made in the ground. Add soil to the places where the stone did not rest on the soil or dig away places where the stone made a heavy indentation. Replace the stone. After all the stones are in place, give the path a good soaking with a fine spray of water.

CAUTION

ESTABLISHING A WALKABLE SURFACE

Although a flagstone walkway should look casual and free-form when you are done, try to create an even surface when laying the stones. Use a straight 2×4 to check for rises or valleys. Unless you have extremely firm or claylike soil, it is best to set the flagstones about ¾ inch or so higher than you want them. In time they will settle.

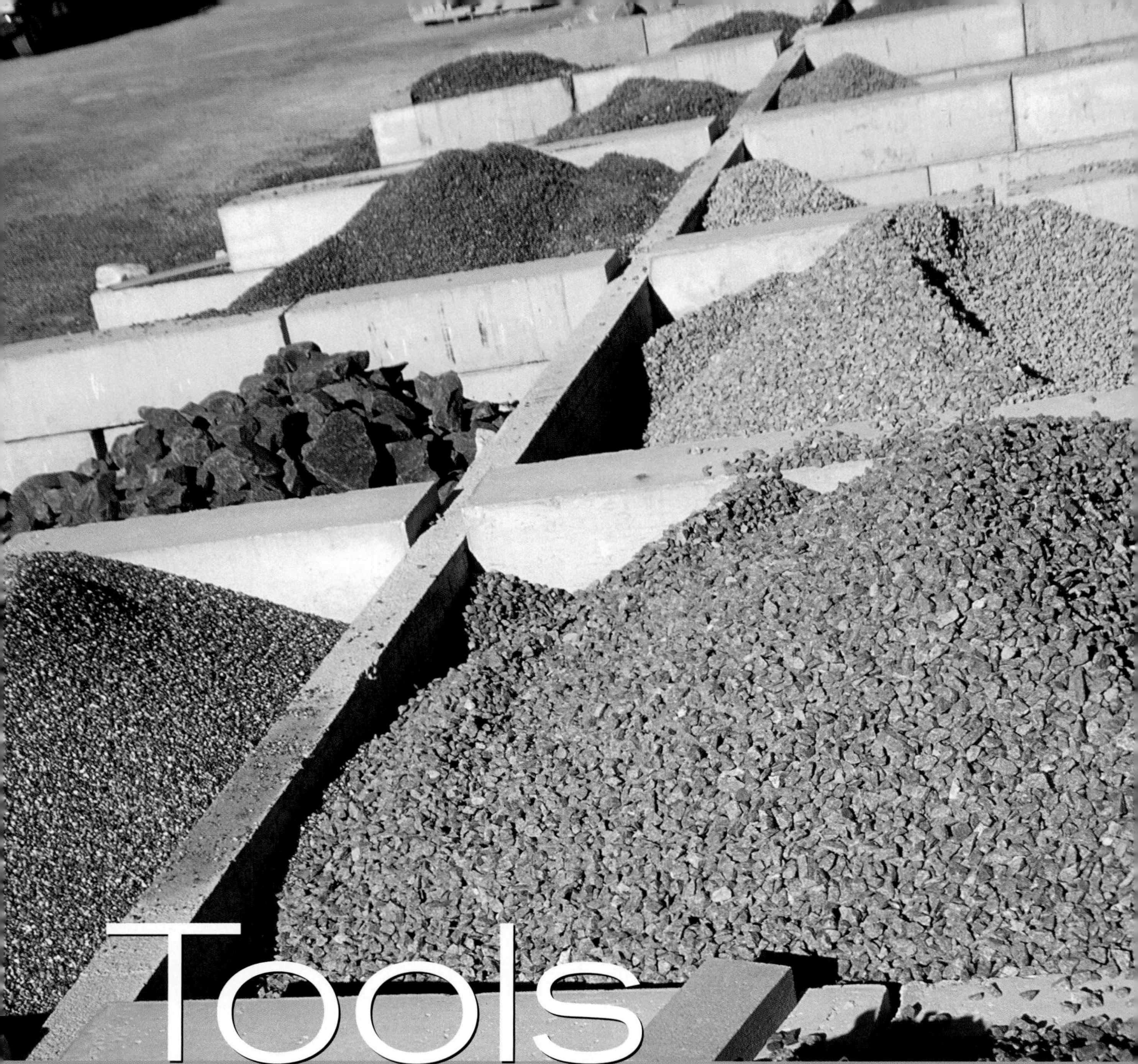

Tools AND MATERIALS

When designing a path, wall, or patio you can choose from a wide selection of products and materials that allows you to build with a distinctive flair. A stroll through the aisles of home centers, lumberyards, and construction material suppliers can be overwhelming. When you see something that interests you, ask questions about it. If you're unsure what will be required to install the material, ask. Be realistic about the complexity of a project; you may find you will need special tools or equipment to place the material.

STONE CHOICES
You can choose from a variety of crushed rock colors, types, and sizes to build a surface that drains well but requires only minimum maintenance.

ASSEMBLING TOOLS AND MATERIALS
Specialized tools and materials make patio construction easier. A bricklayer's hammer is handy for driving steel spikes to anchor preformed edging, as well as cutting bricks.

COLORFUL BRICKS
Consider the variations available in each type of patio material. Here bricks of slightly different colors work together to create a visually interesting design.

PLENTIFUL PAVERS
Precast concrete pavers such as these are available in a wide range of colors, shapes, and sizes. Choose pavers with a high strength rating to withstand the elements over time.

SELECTING MASONRY AND CONCRETE TOOLS

Successful masonry and concrete work requires special techniques. Having the correct tools is essential if you want straight mortar lines and smooth surfaces. Compared with carpentry tools, masonry tools are not expensive, so don't hesitate to buy the best tools. Cheap tools can make the job more difficult and lead to shoddy-looking work that you'll have to live with for a long time. If your budget is tight, consider renting professional-quality tools rather than buying something from the bargain bin.

A circular saw, framing square, tape measure, chalk line, line level, and 4-foot level are general-purpose tools you'll need. For mixing and transporting masonry materials and concrete, get a sturdy contractor-quality wheelbarrow with a capacity of at least 3 cubic feet. Make sure the tire is air-filled. A mortar box is handy for mixing large amounts of cement or mortar, and a mortar hoe allows you to mix materials more easily than a garden hoe or a shovel.

To prepare the site and move concrete and mortar ingredients, you'll need a round-point shovel for general digging, a square-blade shovel for moving sand and wet concrete, and a spade for squaring up a slab excavation or a footing trench.

Use a tamper to prepare soil for masonry surfaces. The beginning steps in finishing concrete require a darby, a wood or magnesium float, and/or a bull float. For final finishing use a steel finishing trowel. An edger is necessary to round off and strengthen edges of slabs. Make control joints with a groover while the material is still wet, or cut the joints after concrete is set using a circular saw with a masonry blade.

Cutting bricks, blocks, or stones is easier if you use a brick set or masonry chisel and a bricklayer's hammer or a 2-pound small sledgehammer.

When building concrete or masonry walls, you'll need line blocks, line clips, a mason's line, a modular spacing rule, and a plumb bob (a chalk line can be used in place of a plumb bob).

For placing mortar use a well-balanced pointed brick trowel. Use a pointing trowel, ⅜-inch back filler, or a sled jointer to force mortar into joints being repaired (tuckpoint). Finish the joints with a concave jointer; these are available in different shapes and help you finish (strike) mortar joints between bricks, blocks, or stones. A good, stiff hand brush is necessary for finishing the job, along with a variety of stiff brushes for cleanup.

If you finish the concrete with a nonskid surface, have handy a stiff-bristled push broom. To cure concrete you need a garden hose with an adjustable nozzle or an oscillating lawn sprinkler.

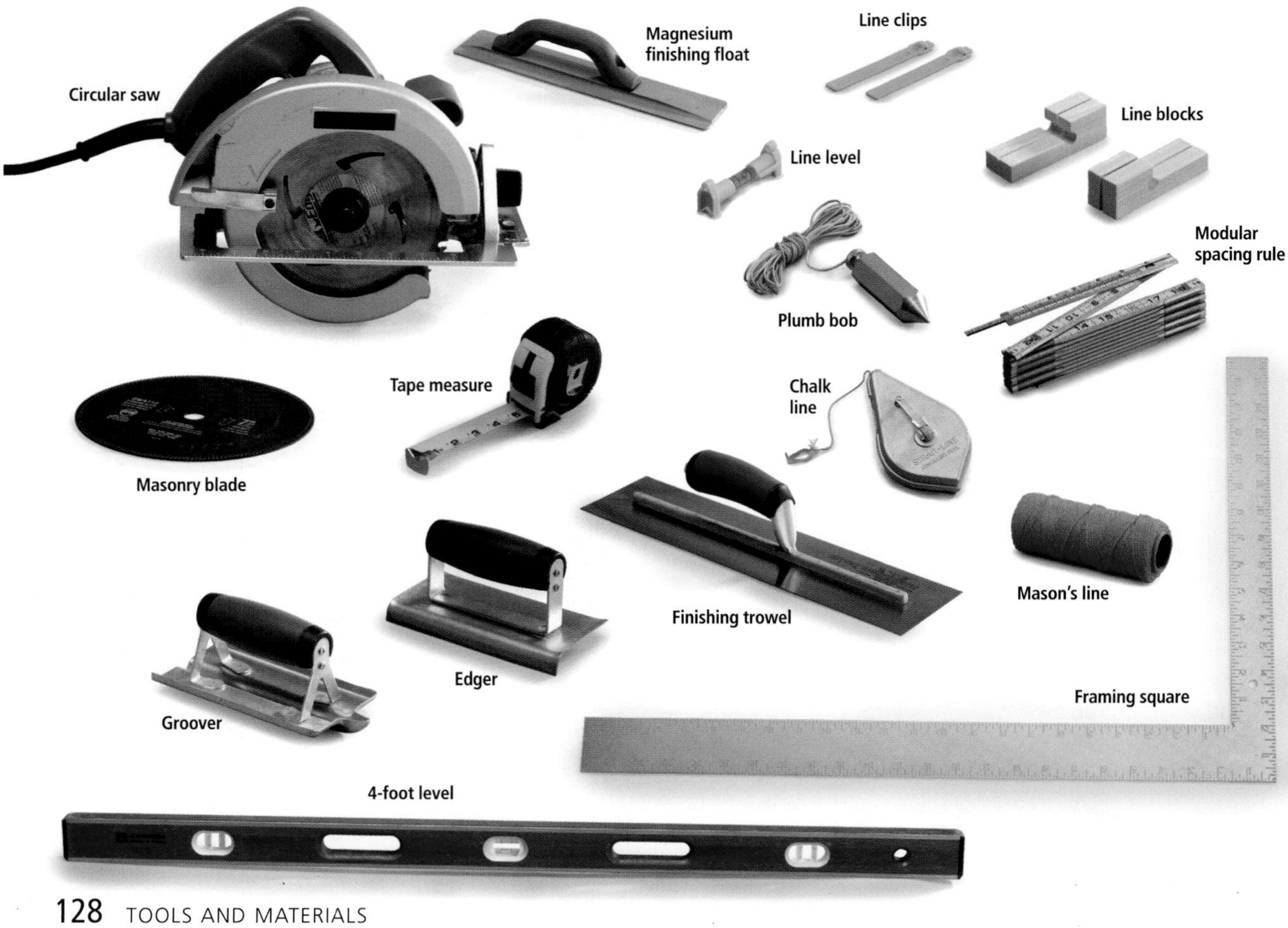

Wood float
Bull float
(magnesium)
Tamper
Darby
Brick set
Small sledgehammer
Bricklayer's hammer
Round-point shovel
Hand brush
Masonry chisel
Square-blade shovel
Spade
3/8" tuck pointer
Brick trowel
Pointing trowel
Concave jointer
Sled jointer
Wheelbarrow
Mortar hoe
Mortar box

SELECTING WALL MATERIALS

Brick

Manufactured by firing molded clay or shale, bricks vary widely in color, texture, and dimensions. Despite these variations, they fall into four main categories: common or building, paver, fire, and facing.

Bricks are modular, meaning that they are either one-half or one-third as wide as they are long. The most common nominal modular unit is 4 inches. Like lumber, bricks are described according to nominal rather than actual sizes. For instance, the actual size of a 4×8 brick is 3⅝×7⅝ inches. The nominal size is the actual size plus a normal mortar joint of ⅜ to ½ inch on the bottom and at one end.

For outdoor projects that must withstand moisture and freeze-thaw cycles, ask for SW (severe-weathering-grade) bricks. For indoor uses, such as facing a fireplace or a planter, you can use MW (moderate weathering) or NW (no weathering).

BRICK AND MORTAR
This thoughtfully composed patio area features two kinds of brick. The wall was constructed from a light brick that complements the grout used on the patio itself. The patio features a slightly more rustic reddish brick.

Stone

Building stone is divided into three basic types: rubble, flagstone, and ashlar.

Rubble is composed of round rocks of various sizes. Flagstone consists of flat pieces, 2–4 inches thick, of irregular shapes. Ashlar, or dimensioned stone, is cut into pieces of uniform thickness for laying in coursed or noncoursed patterns.

Quarried stone is cut from a mountainside or a pit; fieldstone is rock that has been found lying in fields or along rivers. (See pages 82–85 for how to build stone walls.)

DRY-STACKED FLAGSTONE
Flagstone is a viable option for a low retaining wall such as this one. To create a wall that can double as extra seating space, select large, smooth stones for the top course.

Selecting wall materials *(continued)*

Concrete

Concrete is a mixture of sand, coarse aggregate, portland cement, and water. The sand used in concrete should be blank-run sand, which is fairly round in shape and of various sizes. The coarse aggregate is gravel or crushed stone. Concrete should have aggregate pieces no larger than one-quarter the thickness of the pour. For example, if the pour is less than 4 inches thick, the aggregate should be less than 1 inch in size. Portland cement is made of clay, lime, and other ingredients that have been heated in a kiln and ground into a fine powder. Choose Type 1 cement. See pages 22–49 for how to work with concrete.

MASONRY VENEERS.

Masonry veneers are made of brick, natural or artificial stone, or terra-cotta (unglazed, fired clay). Except in very dry climates, their use should be restricted to interior projects, such as covering concrete or masonry walls or applying a decorative finish over drywall or plaster walls (see pages 104–105).

MORTAR INGREDIENTS.

Essential to all brick and block construction, mortar is a paste made of water, cement, lime, and sand. Lime slows the setting speed, making the mortar easier to work. Mortar by itself is not as strong as concrete, but it has strong adhesive properties. In combination with stone, brick, or block, it creates extra-strong walls. In addition mortar serves as an attractive spacer between materials and helps hide their imperfections. It also has a decorative function. Joints can be tooled to various finishes (see page 147). Mortar also can be pigmented.

ARCHITECTURAL BLOCK.

The shapes, sizes, textures, styles, and colors of concrete masonry have expanded dramatically over the past two decades, and availability is no longer limited to the professional builder. A do-it-yourselfer can draw upon architectural block to create truly unique structures that combine creativity and functionality. Durable, easy to use, and affordable, these blocks are ideal for exterior walls.

CONCRETE BLOCKS AND BRICKS.

Concrete blocks and bricks are cast from a stiff concrete mix and are heavy. (Cinder blocks, made of lightweight clay or pumice, are not as strong.) Hollow cores in the blocks help conserve material, make them easier to grip and place, add insulation value, and provide channels for utilities. Use N-grade blocks for places where a wall will be exposed to freezing, and S-grade blocks where it will be shielded from the weather.

A typical stretcher concrete block—the most commonly used block—has a nominal size of 8×8×16 inches and weighs about 45 pounds. Corner blocks have finished edges. A bundle of blocks usually has a mixture of stretchers and corners. Use caps to finish off exposed tops of block walls. Mortarless blocks are laid on top of each other without mortar joints. Once the wall is stacked in place, you reinforce it and grout it.

INTERLOCKING CONCRETE BLOCK.

The easiest way for do-it-yourselfers to design and build retaining walls is using mortarless interlocking concrete blocks. And with a variety of types available from material suppliers and major home centers, you can find a system that is right for the job and meets your design needs as well. Manufacturers cast blocks in various shapes, colors, and textures to give them the look of natural stone. Some interlocking systems include corner and cap blocks. Cast blocks shaped specifically for serpentine walls are also available.

Installation techniques vary. Some manufacturers interlock blocks using pins. Others use clips or joints cast into the block itself. A popular interlocking style is to place a flange on the back of the block so each course is stepped back slightly from the one below to create a batter angle. Once you provide the base foundation (see pages 86–87), you set the interlocking blocks.

NO MORTAR REQUIRED
Interlocking blocks do not need mortar. They are held together by various methods, including interlocking flanges, grooves, holes, and pins. Some types can be filled with gravel or concrete for even greater strength. Interlocking blocks are ideal for building raised planting beds or retaining walls (see pages 86–87).

SELECTING SURFACE MATERIALS

Stone

Use stone materials where you want a rugged look in exterior walls, borders, and patio surfaces. Most of the cost of stone is in transporting it.

If you live near a field or river that has large, attractive stones, you may be able to find, rather than buy, fieldstone. Be sure to get permission from the landowner to take stones, and protect your back when lifting.

Flagstone and stone tile are the most commonly used stones for patio surfaces. Stone tile is cut as precisely as other tile. Slate is suitable for interior floors; only in mild climates can it be used for exterior surfaces. Slate can be purchased randomly cut or as "Vermont tile," which comes in boxes containing the exact tiles for a patchwork-style pattern.

Tile and block

Tiles come in many colors, shapes, and sizes for exterior use. Though they are expensive, you can reduce the cost by using tile as an accent for other flooring treatments.

Adobe, once limited to use in the Southwest and subject to rapid decay, is now reinforced with asphalt and is suitable for all types of climates.

Tile comes in a wide variety of shapes, colors, and textures. To avoid a slippery surface, choose unglazed tiles for exterior use. Tiles that are ¾ inch or more thick can be set in sand for exterior surfaces (see pages 17 and 62–65). Thinner tiles should be set in mortar on a solid concrete base for patios or used only on interior floors (see pages 74–75).

Turf block, made of strong cast concrete, can be set directly on top of smooth, well-tamped soil. Grass grows right through turf block. Its grid configuration provides excellent drainage.

Concrete pavers

Concrete pavers are extremely popular because of their low cost and durability; they will outlast any patio material except stone. Some people feel that concrete pavers lack the warmth of stone or tile and like imitation brick. Today's advanced manufacturing techniques, however, have made it difficult to tell the imitations from the real thing.

The advantages of precast concrete pavers include aesthetic appeal, durability of color, and wide range of styles. Their ability to withstand the freeze-thaw cycles of many regions makes them attractive for use no matter where you live.

Pavers are relatively easy to install (see pages 62–65 and 68–69). They can be set to allow for some drainage between their joints. Several interlocking patterns are available. Colors include pink, gray, and a reddish brown. Some have exposed aggregate surfaces. Higher-priced pavers come close to the color of stone or adobe, often by slightly varying the colors from stone to stone. Pavers also can be custom-pigmented. Grass pavers have an open-grid shape for planting grass or other groundcover.

Concrete pavers

PAVER PATIO
Mixing several geometric shapes in various shades gives this patio the appearance of being constructed of cut stone. Pavers can be dry-set in a sand bed or set on a slab with a mortar base.

Selecting surface materials *(continued)*

Brick

Exterior brick comes in many grades and styles. Two of the most common grades are moderate weathering (MW) and severe weathering (SW). MW bricks, though less expensive, are more porous and typically less uniform in size than SW bricks. Because it is porous, MW brick absorbs water. A freeze-thaw cycle will take its toll, causing the brick to crack and chip over time. SW bricks are constructed to withstand temperature extremes. Because they are less porous, they weather freeze-thaw cycles well and are more resistant to stains.

Styles include common brick, paving brick, used or salvaged brick, and clinker bricks. Common brick, though generally used for walls, can be used for walkways that don't carry a lot of traffic. Paving brick withstands high-traffic use because it is made with denser clay and fired to a higher temperature. Used or salvaged brick has a worn, rustic look that many find attractive, but its uneven surface limits its use mostly to accents. Clinkers result from improper firing that creates irregular shapes, scorching, and pits. Clinkers provide an inexpensive alternative for decorative borders or accents.

PAVER PATIO
Defining space with materials affords the luxury of maintaining an open atmosphere. This enclosed outdoor room with adobe walls uses mortared light brick placed in a running pattern to open the shaded space. The patio is set in a sand bed with a basket-weave pattern to allow for drainage of rainwater.

TIMELESS BEAUTY
Weathered pavers provide a natural look for this Southwest desert patio. Set in a sand bed to drain the occasional rain shower, the floor has the feel that it is not only part of the natural landscape, but it also has been around for ages.

Wood chips | Bark | Straw | Pine needles

Mulch

Use mulch to create an intimate, path-less-traveled feeling. It's quick, easy, and less expensive than most materials, especially if you use locally available mulch. Durability depends on the material—some, such as pine straws, readily break down, whereas others, such as some types of bark, take longer to decompose. One maintenance drawback is that you will need to replenish the mulch periodically. The feel underfoot greatly varies; some types, such as coarse bark, can be difficult to walk on. See page 71 for information about installing mulch and other loose materials.

Loose materials

Small stones and pebbles can be used for borders or patio areas that do not receive heavy traffic. They are easy to install: Just excavate the area, lay weed block fabric, set edging, pour in the material, and rake it smooth (see page71). Once tamped down, these materials form a stable surface and offer a little cushion for comfortable walking.

Choose materials that complement your patio, deck, or yard. Suppliers usually have large bins of different kinds from which to choose. Crushed granite, redrock, and quartz pebbles compact well but usually have sharp edges that can hurt bare feet. River rocks are smooth and handsome-looking but make an uncomfortable walking surface and are slippery when wet.

FIGURING CONCRETE NEEDS

With the help of a calculator, you can determine how much concrete you need. Suppliers measure and sell concrete by the yard, which means one cubic yard (3×3×3 feet, or 27 cubic feet).

Measure the project accurately, especially the depth of slabs and any variations in the excavation. A large slab that is only ½ inch thicker than you think it is will need a lot more concrete than your calculation. Double-check the figures with a concrete supplier—you both have an interest in getting the measurement right.

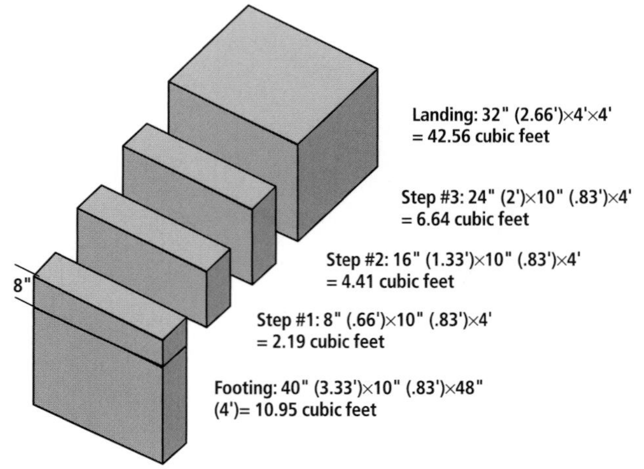

CALCULATE FOR STEPS AND FOOTINGS.

To estimate concrete needs, divide odd-shape jobs into easy-to-figure sections. Add the results to get total volume. In this example the steps have 8-inch (.66-foot) risers and 10-inch (.83-foot) treads, and the landing is 4×4 feet. (To get the number of feet, divide inches by 12.) Use this formula: Length times width times depth equals volume. The sum of the volumes of the footing, landing, and steps is about 67 cubic feet. Assuming you'll fill the forms about two-thirds full of rubble (see page 40), you need about 22 cubic feet of concrete. If you add in a 10-percent cushion, you get 25 cubic feet. Divide that by 27 (the cubic feet in a cubic yard), and your estimate is a bit less than 1 cubic yard.

To find the area of a cylindrical pier, square the radius and multiply by 3.14, then multiply by the depth of the pier.

CAUTION

DON'T UNDERESTIMATE

Nothing is worse than finding out that you are a few cubic feet short of having enough concrete. Adding more after the first batch has set will weaken the final product. Aim for buying a little more than you need.

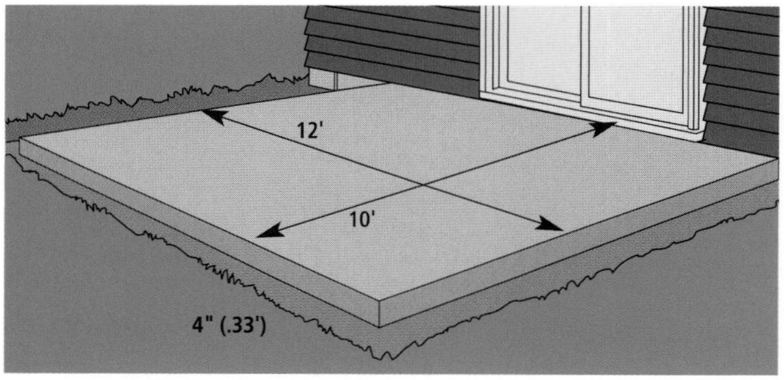

CALCULATE FOR A SLAB.

To estimate concrete for a rectangular slab, multiply width times length times depth. In the slab shown, this is 10×12×.33 feet = 39.6, which rounds up to 40 cubic feet. Add 10 percent for a cushion and divide by 27, and you find that you need 1⅔ cubic yards. For a circular slab, determine the area in square feet by squaring the radius of the circle (half the diameter) and multiplying by 3.14. Then multiply by the depth of the slab to determine the volume in cubic feet. Divide by 27 and add 10 percent for excavation variation.

CONCRETE ESTIMATOR

Concrete required in yards or cubic feet by surface area of job in square feet

Slab Thickness	20	50	100	200	500
4 inches	.2 (6.7)	.6 (16.7)	1.2 (33.3)	2.5 (66.7)	6.2 (166.7)
6 inches	.4 (10)	.9 (25)	1.9 (50)	3.7 (100)	9.3 (250)
8 inches	.5 (13.3)	1.3 (33.3)	2.5 (66.6)	5.9 (133.3)	12.5 (333.3)

BUYING AND MIXING CONCRETE

You can buy concrete three different ways. For small jobs, such as setting a few fence posts, buy bags of premixed concrete that you mix with water. Premix comes in bags weighing up to 80 pounds and contains cement, sand, and aggregate mixed together. Each bag contains enough mixture to make about ⅔ cubic foot. For jobs that require ½ cubic yard or more, it's best to order ready-mix concrete delivered in a truck. This is much easier than mixing your own, and you will be assured of a reliable mix.

If you have a large job that requires you to work in small stages, it makes sense to buy cement, sand, and aggregate, and mix your own concrete. In a wheelbarrow, large trough, or machine mixer, mix 10 shovelfuls of portland cement, 22 shovelfuls of sand, and 30 shovelfuls of aggregate for each cubic foot of concrete. Making small batches allows you to place and finish one section at a time.

The ideal temperature for working concrete is 70 degrees. Warmer or colder temperatures hasten or retard the rate of setting and curing. Avoid working in severe cold; freezing can ruin uncured concrete.

ON-SITE MIXING TRUCKS

Standard concrete trucks carry concrete that has been mixed at the company's site; thus, the supplier will be reluctant to sell less than a yard of concrete. A new innovation is a delivery truck that mixes the concrete right at the site. Usually this is more economical for smaller amounts of concrete.

Mixing concrete

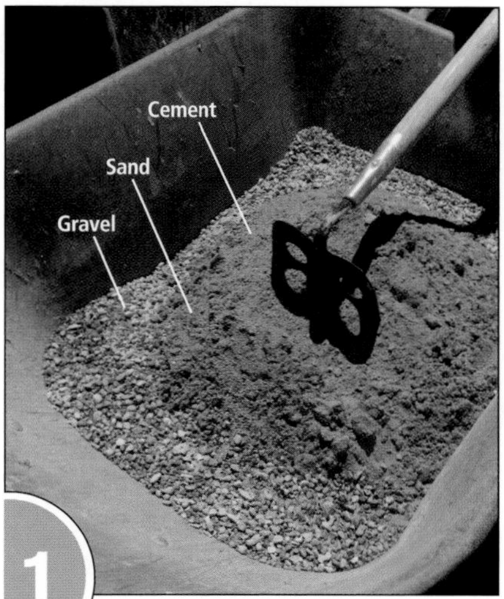

1 LAYER THE INGREDIENTS AND COMBINE.

Shovel the gravel, sand, and cement in the order shown to achieve a consistent mix in the shortest time. This way it is less likely that the finer ingredients will settle to the bottom. Mix together the dry ingredients with a mortar hoe before adding water.

2 MIX IN THE WATER.

Add small amounts of water to the dry mix, and stir it thoroughly with a mortar hoe. Eventually it will take on the consistency of mud. When it turns a uniform shiny gray color, the mixture is close to the correct consistency; test it using the procedure in Step 3.

CONCRETE MIXING PROPORTIONS

Coarse Aggregate
Use ¾- to 1-inch gravel
40-50 percent

Sand
40-50 percent

(Coarse aggregate and sand together) = 1½ tons*

Cement
Use five 94-pound bags of portland cement** for concrete strong enough to withstand 3,000 pounds per square inch (PSI) or six bags to withstand 3,500 psi*** = 1 cubic yard of concrete

* These ingredients can be purchased separately or together in a mixture.

** The more cement, the stronger the mix.

*** For projects requiring extra lateral strength, such as a driveway.

3 TEST THE CONSISTENCY.

Smack the concrete with the back of your shovel. Chop it to create a groove about 2 inches deep. If the groove maintains its shape, you've got the right mixture. If the groove is indistinct, add water. If the groove caves in, add more dry ingredients.

Solving PROBLEMS

Time and the elements eventually wear down even granite mountains. Seemingly indestructible brick, concrete, and pavers will deteriorate under the same elements. Most of the wear can be repaired, but some requires replacement. In this section you will find information about fixing and replacing concrete, bricks, steps, chimneys, and asphalt surfaces. Also included are instructions for repairing basement leaks and railings.

CHIMNEY CHARM
The whitewash finish of the chimney fits the aesthetic of this tidy cottage. Read about chimney maintenance on pages 150–151.

CONCRETE CHORES
Maintaining your dream home involves more than upkeep of the foliage. Eventually you will need to patch concrete, or at least remove stains, to keep your home looking its best.

BEAUTY OF BRICK
Brick offers a welcoming touch of class to this home entryway. Replacement of brick may not be in the immediate future, but nature will wear down and eventually crack the brick. It's important to know how to repair and replace it.

SCRUBBING STAINS
The natural stone path along the front of this brick cottage—or the brick itself—may eventually suffer from efflorescence and stain. Settling of stones and cracking from wear will require resetting and replacement.

PATCHING HOLES IN CONCRETE

For spalled (flaking) surfaces or for hairline cracks and small broken areas, use the patch materials discussed in the chart on page 143. If your concrete surface is badly settled and cracked, however, remove the damaged section and pour new concrete. Concrete patches rarely blend in, so if you are concerned with appearance, you may want to replace entire sections regardless of the extent of the damage.

YOU'LL NEED

TIME: About 1–2 hours for several small patches; a full day to remove and repour a section.

SKILLS: Chiseling, mixing concrete, finishing concrete.

TOOLS: Masonry chisel, small sledgehammer, brush, finishing trowel, mixing trough or wheelbarrow.

CHECK OUT CRACKING

Spalling or cracking in an old slab may be caused by freeze-thaw cycles or settling of the ground under the slab.

If a slab less than three years old is spalling, the concrete probably was mixed incorrectly. More flaking likely will occur in the future. Serious cracks can result from a weak mix, the failure to install reinforcing metal where needed, or unstable ground beneath the slab. Your best bet is to tear up the concrete and start again.

1 TO REPAIR A SPALLED AREA, "KEY" THE HOLE WITH A CHISEL.

All around the damaged area, hold a masonry chisel at an angle and pound it with a small sledgehammer to remove the top ½–1 inch of the concrete surface. "Key" the hole by undercutting the edges so the bottom of the hole is larger than the top. This helps lock the new patching material into the old concrete, making a permanent bond.

2 CLEAN AND DAMPEN THE HOLE.

Brush out dust and small particles. If any of the area surrounding the hole appears loose, remove it as well. Wet the hole with water, but don't leave any standing water. You may want to apply a latex bonding agent to the area to ensure that the new material adheres to the old surface.

3 POUR AND FINISH THE PATCH.

Mix the patching compound and pour it in. Tamp it firmly in place to make sure all areas are firmly in contact and there are no air bubbles in the material. To allow for shrinkage, mound the patching compound slightly higher than the surrounding surface. Finish with a steel trowel.

CONCRETE PATCHES

Type	Uses	Description and Mixing Instructions
Latex, Vinyl, and Epoxy Patch	General-purpose repair jobs, such as filling hairline cracks, repairing small breaks and patches, and tuckpointing small areas. Latex and epoxy are best for patio surfaces.	Sold in powdered form with or without a liquid binder. Mix with the appropriate binder, usually a sticky white liquid, to a whipped-cream consistency. Mixing any product with a latex reinforcer makes it stronger, as will adding extra portland cement to concrete.
Hydraulic Cement	Plug water leaks in masonry walls and floor surfaces. This fast-drying formulation allows you to make the repair even while the water is leaking in.	Available in powdered form. Mix a small amount with water or a commercial binder, then work quickly.
Dry Premixed Concrete	Use wherever you need to replace whole sections of concrete.	Mix with water. The thicker the consistency, the faster it sets up.

RENT AN ELECTRIC HAMMER

If you're faced with demolishing a 2- or 3-inch-thick concrete slab, try breaking it up with a sledgehammer, as shown below left. If the slab is thick or if the going gets rough, however, don't take the chance of throwing out your back.

Call a rental center and explain your situation. The center should have an electric jackhammer that will help you break up the slab without the strain. (You won't need a pneumatic jackhammer unless you have an extra-large job.) Whatever method you use, wear eye and ear protection; wear gloves for handling broken concrete.

1 FOR A LARGER SECTION, REMOVE DAMAGED CONCRETE.

Use a brick set or masonry chisel and a small sledgehammer to score the bottom of the control joints (grooves) that separate the damaged section from adjacent ones. This will prevent random cracking beyond the joint.

Break out pieces by hammering at the same spot with an 8- or 10-inch maul until the concrete fractures. Using a sledgehammer, break it into pieces small enough to lift without strain. Use pieces of rubble, as shown in the inset, to break large pieces apart. Carefully chip away final areas along the control joints. Then clear away the waste.

2 FORM AND POUR A NEW SLAB.

Chop out any roots; they may have been the cause of your problem. Install forms and expansion material, as shown above, and spread sand or crushed rock to fill in low spots in the subgrade. Tamp the whole area firmly. Lay in reinforcing wire mesh to within 2 inches of the form's edges. Position the mesh midway, vertically, in the slab by laying it on pieces of small debris or rubble. Pour concrete mix in the form and finish it (see pages 40–45). Duplicate the finish texture of the existing concrete as closely as possible.

REPAIRING BASEMENT LEAKS

Basement leaks make life miserable, and they can weaken the foundation of your home. Basement walls should seal out a moderate amount of water, but few will withstand a great deal of water pressure. If the wall leaks only during heavy rains, you may be able to solve the problem by adding extensions to your gutter downspouts to direct rainwater away from the basement walls. You may find that your yard slopes in a way that causes rainwater to flow toward your home. If so, some corrective landscaping may solve your problem.

YOU'LL NEED

TIME: Several hours for most small patching jobs; several days or more if you need to seal the outside of the wall.

SKILLS: No special skills needed.

TOOLS: Stiff brush, masonry chisel, small sledgehammer.

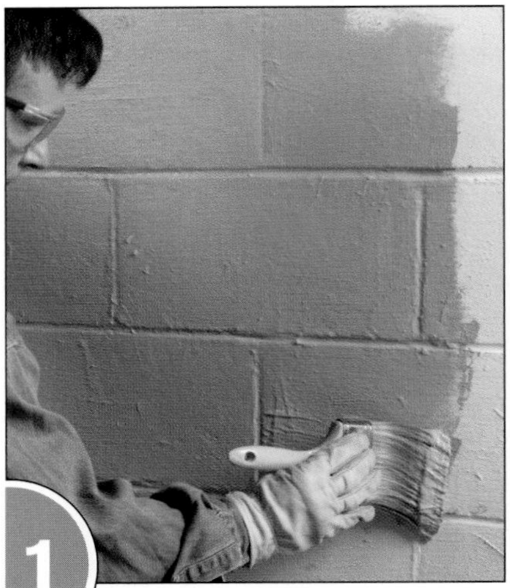

1 BRUSH ON SEALER.

If the problem is slow seepage or damp walls, use an interior sealer. Clean away dirt, grease, and dust from the wall. If you are using a cement-based sealing product, wet the wall thoroughly with a fine mist from a garden hose. Mix the liquid and powder components of the sealer thoroughly. Apply with a stiff brush.

2 FILL ANY CRACKS.

As you brush be sure to fill in all the pores in the wall. Go over cracks several times to fill them.
If a crack is too large to fill in with sealer, use hydraulic cement (see below). With some sealers you must keep the sealant wet for several days to ensure bonding. Apply a second coat if necessary.

1 "KEY" THE CRACK.

Enlarge a hole or crack with a masonry chisel and hammer. Undercut it to make a "key," so the plug won't come loose. Make the hole at least ½ inch deep. Use a whisk broom to brush out fragments of concrete and dust.

2 MIX THE CEMENT.

In a bucket add water to the dry hydraulic cement mix until it has a puttylike consistency. Then work it by hand. For a hole, roll it into the shape of a plug. Roll a long snake shape for a crack.

3 APPLY THE CEMENT.

Squeeze the roll into the opening. Keep pushing and pushing to make sure it fills every tiny crevice. If water was leaking through the wall at the time of the repair, it should stop. Hold the material in place for several minutes to allow the patch to set.

WATER ABSORPTION

Problem	Symptoms/Tests	Causes	Solutions
Condensation	Damp walls, dripping pipes, rusty hardware, mildew. To identify condensation, tape a mirror in the dampest spot and wait 24 hours. If it's foggy or beaded with water, condensation is the problem.	Excess humidity in the air, usually from an internal source, such as a basement shower, washing machine, or unvented dryer, or from a significant difference between the wall temperature and inside air temperature.	Install a dehumidifier, improve ventilation, and seal interior walls.
Seepage	Dampness on a section of a wall or floor, most often on a wall near floor level. Tape a mirror to the wall. If moisture condenses behind it, seepage is the culprit.	Surface water is forcing its way through pores in the foundation or an expansion joint. The source may be poor drainage or a leaky window well.	Improve exterior drainage. If the problem is minor, an interior sealer may work. If not, waterproof the outside of the foundation.
Leaks	Localized wetness that seems to be oozing or even trickling from a wall or floor. It usually appears during heavy rain. Test by running a hose outside near the leak. Pay particular attention to mortar joints between blocks.	Cracks that may result from normal settling or improperly poured concrete. (If you see a cracklike line running horizontally around your basement wall, it may be that the builders poured part of the wall and allowed it to harden before pouring the rest.) Faulty roof drainage or a grade that slopes toward the wall exacerbates the problem.	Improve exterior drainage. You may be able to plug several holes. For widespread leakage, waterproof the entire foundation and install drain tile.
Subterranean water	A thin, barely noticeable film of water on the basement floor is often the first sign. Test by laying down plastic sheeting for two days. Penetrating moisture will dampen the concrete underneath.	Usually a spring or a high water table forces water up from below under high pressure, turning your basement into a well. This may happen only during rainy periods.	Install a sump pump. Drainage tile around the perimeter of the foundation may help, but only if it drains to a low spot or a storm sewer.

1 TO SEAL A WALL FROM THE OUTSIDE, EXCAVATE TO THE TROUBLE AREA.

If the problem is fairly high up on the foundation wall, you may be able to do the digging yourself. Otherwise hire an excavating contractor to backhoe a trench wide enough for you to work in. Remove the dirt close to the wall by hand. Brush the wall clean.

2 APPLY SEALER.

You can hire contractors who specialize in this type of coating. To do it yourself, wash the wall clean, allow it to dry, and apply two coats of tar-like bituminous sealer. Or back-plaster the wall with two coats of mortar and then apply the sealer.

3 INSTALL A DRAINPIPE AND BARRIER.

Dig a trench along the footing and install a sloping, perforated drainpipe embedded in gravel (see page 83). Stick heavy-gauge polyethylene sheeting to the wall sealer. Drape it over the footing, but not the gravel drain. Overlap all seams at least 6 inches.

PATCHING CRACKS AND TUCKPOINTING

Even well-built masonry walls require occasional repairs. Mortar joints that are exposed to the weather typically need to be tuckpointed every 30 years or so.

Cracking, the most common masonry malady, results from uneven settling of footings or from expansion and contraction due to temperature changes. Expansion cracks usually occur with uniform width and often follow joints between bricks or blocks. Settling cracks taper along a mostly vertical path, are widest at the top, and end as hairline cracks near the bottom of the wall.

Horizontal cracking may appear in basement walls made of concrete blocks. Usually the cause is pressure from backfill soil and water pushing in from the outside. If the wall bulges noticeably, you have a serious problem. You may need to dig out the backfill and re-lay the blocks—a job best handled by a professional.

The same procedures are used for repairing a cracked mortar line and for tuckpointing. For a long-lasting tuckpointing job, chisel or grind out all the joints. If your grout lines generally are worn and cracking, you need to tuckpoint the entire area or the problem will worsen rapidly.

Tuckpointing is painstaking, slow work. It can be done from a ladder, but you'll find the work easier, and you'll do a better job, if you set up scaffolding.

YOU'LL NEED

TIME: About two hours to tuckpoint 25 square feet of wall.

SKILLS: Working with mortar.

TOOLS: Jointing tool of your choice, ⅜-inch pointing trowel, masonry chisel, small sledgehammer, stiff brush, whisk broom.

1

CHISEL OUT THE JOINTS…

With a small sledgehammer and a masonry chisel, remove mortar from joints to a depth of ⅜–1 inch. It is possible to tuckpoint without chiseling out old mortar, but the tuckpointing will not last as long. Because chips will fly as you work, wear safety goggles and heavy gloves.

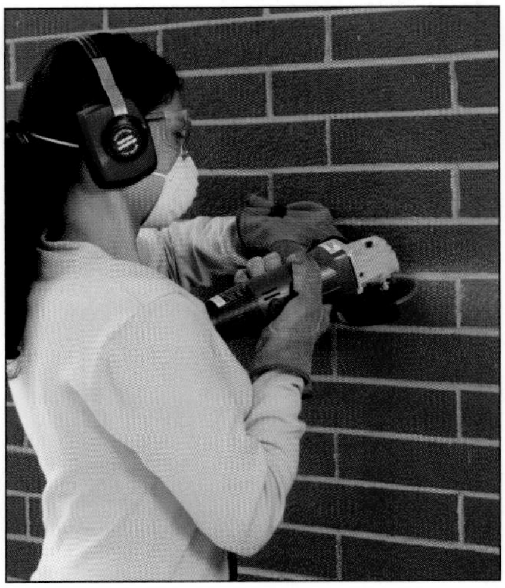

OR USE A GRINDER.

If you need to work on a large area, rent or purchase a 4-inch grinder to efficiently remove old mortar. Whichever method you use, if the joint crumbles easily all the way through the wall, tear down the whole section and re-lay the bricks with new mortar. Tuckpointing by itself will not add strength to weak masonry joints.

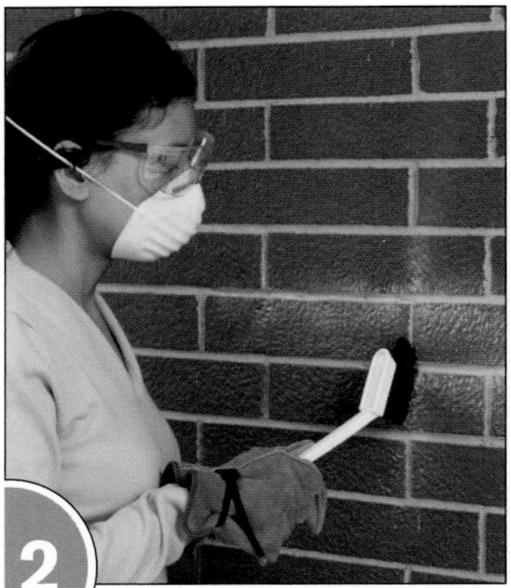

2

SCRAPE AND BRUSH OUT DEBRIS.

Use the point of a masonry chisel or the tip of a pointed trowel to scrape away patches of mortar that remain after chiseling or grinding. Sweep away debris. Mix the mortar using 1 part portland cement to 2 parts masonry sand and enough water to form a puttylike consistency (page 97).

WAIT FOR WALL MOVEMENT TO STOP

To repair wall cracks caused by settling, you must wait until the movement stops before patching or tuckpointing. This may be as long as a year after the first signs of cracking appear.

To determine if settling still is occurring, bridge the crack with a piece of duct tape and check it occasionally for twists, tears, or pulling loose.

3 PLACE THE MORTAR.

Load an upside-down trowel with mortar and hold it against the wall. With a ⅜-inch pointing trowel, force the mortar into the joints. Fill the head (vertical) joints first, then the bed (horizontal) joints. It will take practice before you can tuckpoint without dropping mortar or smearing bricks.

4 STRIKE THE JOINTS.

Use a damp sponge to wipe away excess mortar while it is still wet. Brush the joints to remove mortar crumbs. Correct timing is essential for striking the joints. The mortar should be stiff, but not hard. Choose the appearance of your joint from those shown below.

5 RESTRIKE AND BRUSH.

To ensure that your joints are watertight, strike them a second time, making sure they seal tightly against the bricks. Let the mortar set up somewhat, then brush away crumbs with a stiff brush. Scrub mortar stains off the wall within 24 hours.

CHOOSING A MORTAR JOINT

STRUCK JOINT.

Make a struck joint with the edge of a pointed trowel, angling the joint from top to bottom. This is an attractive joint but will collect water on the lower edge.

V-JOINT.

Use a V-shaped jointer or a bent piece of metal to make a V-joint. Strike it quickly after the bricks are laid or the mortar will bunch up. This joint sheds water well.

FLUSH JOINT.

Cut the excess mortar from the face of bricks as you lay them. Because mortar is not compacted, it is not recommended for exterior use.

CONCAVE JOINT.

This is the most common brick joint. Strike it using a piece of pipe or a jointer made for this purpose. It sheds water well and is the easiest to make watertight.

WEATHERED JOINT.

Use a pointed trowel, as with a struck joint, but hold it in the opposite way, angling from bottom to top. It's difficult to make this joint look consistent.

RAKED JOINT.

A raked joint looks great, but it is the weakest and the least water-resistant joint. To strike it, use a trimmed piece of wood or a special jointer.

REPLACING BRICKS AND BLOCKS

A few damaged or deteriorated bricks don't spell doom for a wall. They can be replaced with relative ease. Begin by examining the wall carefully. If the damaged bricks or concrete blocks are directly over or under a door or window, there is a chance the wall could sag if you remove several of them at once. To avoid collapsing a section of wall, replace only a few bricks at a time. Call in a professional mason if you are unsure of yourself.

YOU'LL NEED

TIME: About one hour to replace a brick or a block.

SKILLS: Careful chiseling, mixing mortar, pointing mortar lines.

TOOLS: Small sledgehammer, masonry chisel, drill with masonry bit, pointed trowel, pointing tool.

Replacing bricks

1 CHIP OUT THE OLD BRICK.

Use a small sledgehammer and masonry chisel to chip away the old mortar and brick. Drill a series of holes with a masonry bit to make it easy to break the brick apart and remove the pieces without damaging surrounding bricks. Brush away debris and dampen all surfaces of the cavity.

2 SLIDE IN THE NEW BRICK.

Lay a ½- to 1-inch-deep bed of mortar on the bottom of the cavity. Butter the top and ends of the new brick. Slip the brick in without compressing the bed of mortar. Or use a trowel to help slide it in. Adjust the brick so all the joints are even. Strike the joints to match the rest of the wall.

Replacing blocks

1 REMOVE THE OLD BLOCK FACE.

Unless the entire concrete block is fractured, remove only the damaged face and leave the rest. Use a small sledgehammer and a masonry chisel. It may help to bore a series of holes in the block with a masonry bit.

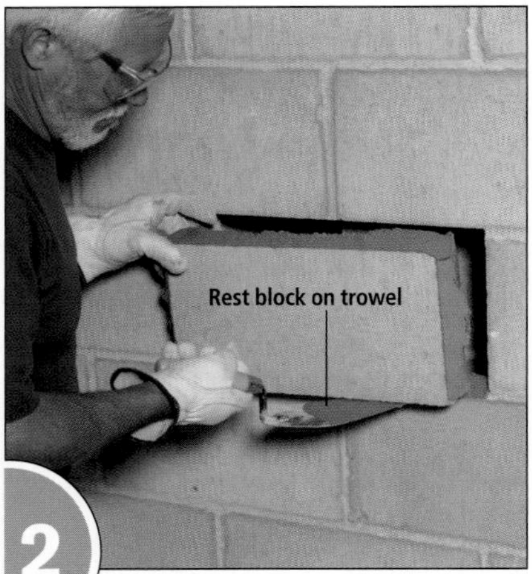

2 SET A NEW BLOCK FACE IN PLACE.

Use a circular saw with a masonry blade to notch the webbing of a new block. Then use a chisel to release one face of the block. Dry-fit the new block face to make sure it is flush with the wall surface. Lay a bed of mortar and butter the block face on three sides. Slip the block in using a pointed trowel.

3 HOLD IN PLACE WITH WEDGES.

The new block face will not stay in place as easily as a new brick, so use wedges to hold it firmly in the correct position. Once the mortar stiffens, remove the wedges, fill in the holes left by the wedges, and strike the joints.

REMOVING EFFLORESCENCE AND STAINS

Efflorescence is a white powder that results when mineral salts in mortar are dissolved by water. These deposits sometimes disappear after a few years. If you want to get rid of them now or if you have other stains or problems, try the techniques listed in the chart at right. As a general rule, try common household cleaners first; use acid only if necessary. Do not use acid on limestone or marble.

CAUTION

Always pour acid slowly into water; never pour water into acid. Wear protective clothing.

YOU'LL NEED

TIME: About two hours to scrub away most stains.

SKILLS: Basic skills.

TOOLS: Protective eyewear, gloves, heavy clothing, stiff brush, water bucket.

REMOVING STAINS

Problem	Remedy
Efflorescence	Try water and a brush and wait a few days. If something stronger is needed, scrub the wall with a solution of 1 part muriatic acid to 15 parts clean water. Rinse with water when finished.
Mortar smears	Remove with a muriatic acid solution as strong as 1 part acid to 10 parts water if your bricks are dark; 1-to-15 solution for lighter bricks. Let stand for 10–15 minutes, then rinse thoroughly.
Mildew	Scrub gently with a solution of 1 part bleach to 3 parts water, with a little laundry detergent or trisodium phosphate mixed in. Let stand for 15 minutes, then rinse.
Hardened paint	Scrape off as much as possible with a putty knife. Scrub with a metal-bristled brush and cold water. If this doesn't work, try a commercial paint remover, but test it on a small spot first to make sure it does not stain the brick.
Graffiti	Purchase a spray-paint remover and follow directions.
Iron rust	Try scrubbing with household bleach, letting it stand for 15 minutes, and rinsing. If that doesn't work, scrub with a solution of 1 pound oxalic acid to 1 gallon of water. Let stand for 5 minutes, then rinse thoroughly. Test on a small area first to make sure it will not stain the brick.

PREVENTION IS KEY

Concrete is a versatile and durable surface that is also porous, soaking up various stains and, in damp areas, collecting mildew. When removing mildew, apply the stain removal solution (see chart), let it stand for 15 minutes, and then rinse the surface thoroughly. Using a garden hose allows you to easily control the water pressure and surface area covered. Allow the surface to dry and check the results. Prevention is the key to maintaining concrete over time. Properly applying a concrete sealer and using a stiff-bristled broom often can help keep mildew to a minimum.

REPAIRING CHIMNEYS

A chimney is susceptible to a number of problems, including the buildup of flammable deposits in the flue and damaged and leaking masonry. Serious damage requires repair by a professional mason. Homeowners willing to get up on the roof can handle basic inspection, repairs, and minor improvements. This section shows the basic steps for inspecting your chimney to keep it in safe working order and some improvements to make future maintenance procedures simple.

YOU'LL NEED

TIME: About two hours to make a yearly inspection; several hours to clean out a chimney.

SKILLS: For most jobs, no special skills needed.

TOOLS: Rope, tuckpointing tools, mason's trowel.

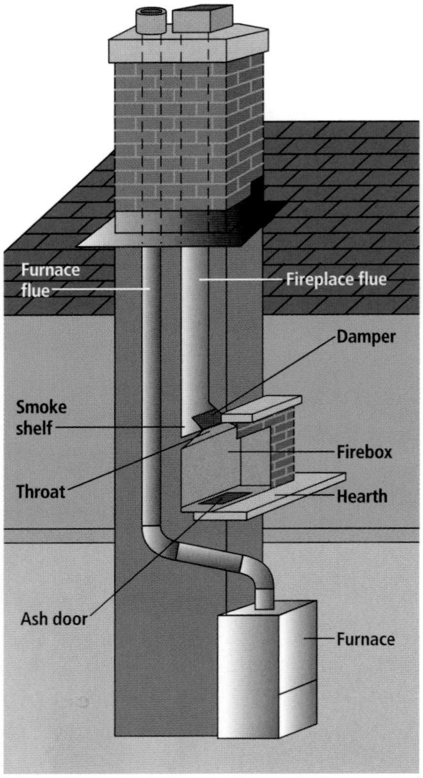

UNDERSTAND CHIMNEY ANATOMY.

The firebox has splayed sides, which pull air across the hearth to the base of the fire. The sloping upper rear wall of the firebox deflects heat back into the room. Above, the throat pulls smoke up into the flue. A damper there allows you to control the draft and close it down when the fireplace is not in use.

Higher up the chimney, a smoke shelf stops cold air from coming down the flue and diverts it back up the flue. Without the smoke shelf, cold air from the outside would drop down and push smoke into the living area. Many fireplaces have an ash door, plus an ash pit and a clean-out door, allowing you to remove your ashes from the outside of the house. Some ash pits have an air vent to create a better draft.

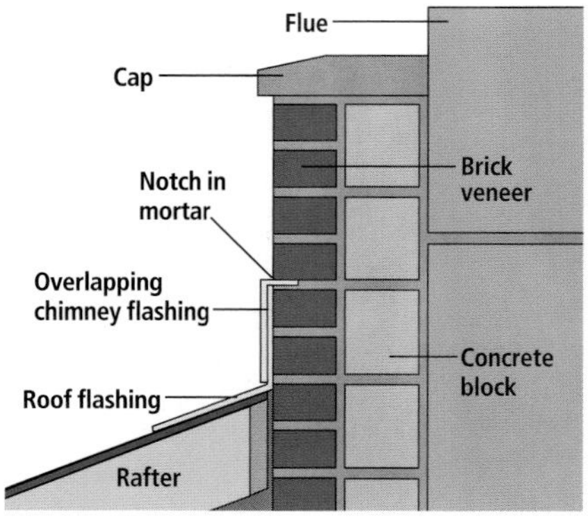

INSPECT THE UPPER CHIMNEY.

The part of a chimney that is exposed to weather is the most likely to fail. Inspect it thoroughly for crumbling bricks and mortar. (Your home's chimney may not look quite like the drawing above; it may be all brick, for instance.) Replace broken bricks and tuckpoint them if necessary (see pages 146–148). Make sure the chimney cap overhangs the brick. Check for loose or missing flashing.

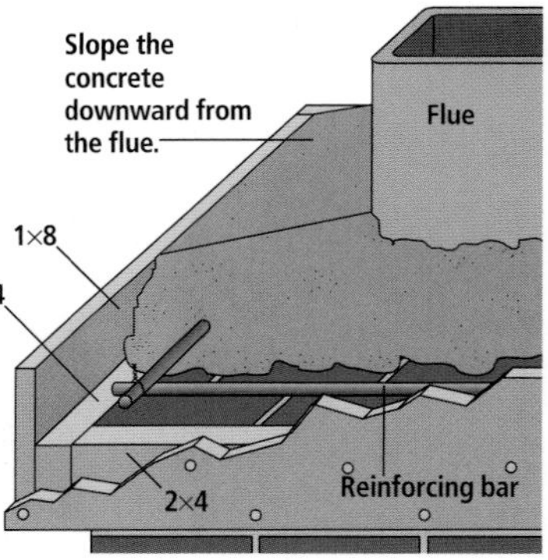

MAKE A NEW CHIMNEY CAP.

Chimney caps often are constructed incorrectly and don't protect the bricks from water damage. Shown here is a design for a cap you can pour in place. Hold the form in place with a few masonry nails and remove it after the concrete has set. When finishing the concrete, be sure to slope it away from the flue so water can run off easily.

CAUTION

AN OUNCE OF PREVENTION

If your fireplace chimney becomes caked with flammable deposits, you could have a flue fire. This is extremely dangerous; the heat is intense, and the fire is difficult to put out. A flue fire can possibly even lead to a house fire. So be sure your chimney is clean before you light a fire.

If your fireplace has not been used for a while, have it examined by a professional who specializes in chimneys.

Your chimney often is connected to the framing of your house. The weight of a damaged chimney can lead to serious structural problems. If you suspect severe damage, call in a professional.

Cleaning a fireplace chimney

SEAL OFF THE INSIDE OPENING.

Cleaning produces a lot of hard-to-vacuum soot, so make sure it cannot enter your home. Tape a wet sheet or a piece of heavy polyethylene sheeting across the opening. Make sure there are no cracks or gaps.

MAKE A "BRUSH."

You can rent or buy a regular chimney brush with extensions for reaching down your chimney. Or make a cleaning tool out of a piece of canvas and a rope. Wrap chains or pieces of broken brick in the canvas, tie a rope to it, and lower it into the flue.

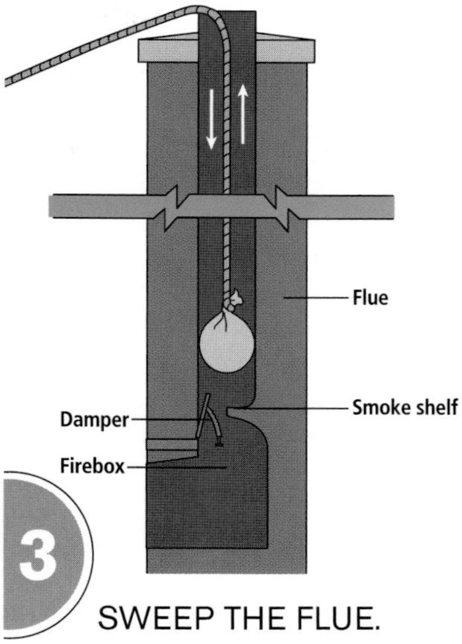

SWEEP THE FLUE.

Move your "brush" vigorously up and down in the flue, slowly moving downward as you work. Lower the brush all the way down to the damper, pull it up, and repeat the process until you no longer hear caked deposits being dislodged from the flue.

AN ANNUAL CHECKUP

Every year make a quick inspection of your chimney:

- See if any tree branches are within 10 feet of the chimney. Trim off the branches if they are; they can cause draw problems and create fire hazards.
- Check that the damper and its controls work smoothly. Use a flashlight to see if it opens and closes completely.
- Test the draw. When you light a fire, the smoke should rise easily and not flow into your living area.
- Clean out ashes that have accumulated in the ash pit.
- On the roof and in the attic, check the chimney bricks and repair any damaged areas.

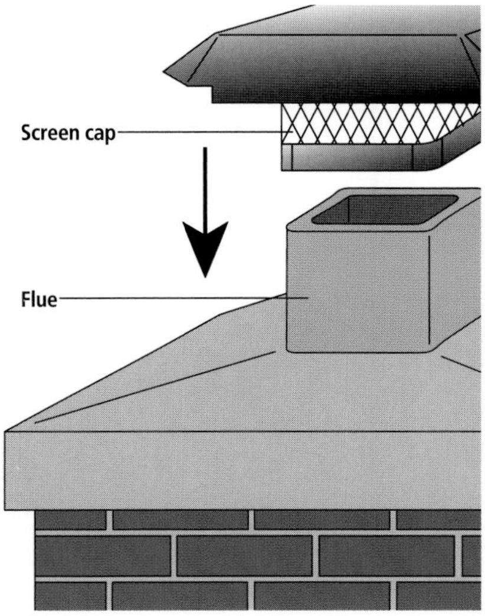

INSTALL A SCREEN CAP.

Keep birds and squirrels out of your chimney and protect the inside from water damage with a screen cap. Measure the outside diameter and purchase a cap to fit. Installation is easy—place it on top of the flue and tighten the hold-down screws.

GAS LOG UNITS

If you want to enjoy a fire in an old fireplace but don't want the cost and work of replacing the entire chimney, consider installing a gas-fired unit. It needs little or no venting, so it does not matter if the chimney draws poorly. And it offers other advantages: You don't have to haul and store logs; it's easy to start; and many slide-in models have circulating systems that efficiently heat a home.

Make sure a chimney poses no structural dangers. Make any needed repairs to ensure it will not collapse or compromise the house framing.

REPAIRING CONCRETE STEPS

Once a crack develops in concrete, water seeps in and causes further damage, especially in regions that have freezing temperatures. Fix small cracks and chips in your stairs right away or you may have to replace the whole set of concrete steps. If your steps are made partially of brick, see pages 146–148 for brick repairs.

Buy patching concrete or concrete sand mix and add extra portland cement. Mix in only enough water to make the material doughlike. If the area is large, drive masonry screws partially into the damaged area to hold the patch in place.

YOU'LL NEED

TIME: About two hours for most repairs.

SKILLS: No special skills needed.

TOOLS: Hammer and masonry chisel, pointed trowel.

REPLACE CHIPS WITH EPOXY CEMENT.

If a piece or two has broken out in such a way that it will fit back in place, you can glue it back on. Clean both pieces and make sure they are dry. Mix epoxy cement, apply it to the chipped-out spot, and brace the chip in place with a brick and a piece of wood.

WHERE THE STEPS MEET THE HOUSE

If you have a crack where your concrete steps butt against the house, any patch you make probably will crack again within a year or two. The steps and the house rest on different foundations, so they shift and settle in different directions. If you don't seal the crack, the problem will get worse. Here's how to seal out moisture and debris.

- If the crack is small, seal it with silicone, butyl rubber, or siliconized acrylic caulk.
- If the crack is large, insert expansion joint material into it for the best seal, or use oakum.

1 TO MEND A BROKEN EDGE, CHIP OUT THE EDGE.

If an edge is broken or cracked, remove all loose material so no cracks remain. With a hammer and masonry chisel, cut the edge back to make a V-shaped groove. Clean the area thoroughly and moisten it.

2 MAKE A FORM AND FILL.

Use bricks to hold a board against the riser to act as a form for the concrete. Mix the patch material and pack it into the groove. Smooth the top of the patch. As the material begins to set up, remove the form and smooth the edges of the patch.

3 CURE THE PATCH SLOWLY.

To ensure that the patch will stick, make sure it cures slowly. Cover the repair with polyethylene sheeting and hold it in place with scraps of lumber. Keep the patched area damp for about a week by spraying it with water.

REPAIRING RAILINGS

Here's a common and pesky problem: The metal railing on a concrete stairway comes loose, either at its base, where it connects to the step, or at the top, where it connects to the house.

Often the problem is rusty metal. If only screws are rusty, you can replace them. If the bottom of the railing itself is rusted away, it may be time for a new railing.

Just as often, the screws or anchors were not large enough for the job and have come loose and possibly cracked the concrete. To make these repairs you can use epoxy putty, anchoring cement, masonry screws, or masonry anchors.

YOU'LL NEED

TIME: About two hours for most repairs.

SKILLS: No special skills needed.

TOOLS: Hammer and masonry chisel, drill with masonry bit, trowel.

1 CHIP AWAY A HOLE.

Remove loose material. Enlarge the hole, if necessary, so it will be deep enough for the new bolt and so the epoxy putty or anchoring cement has plenty of area to grab onto. "Key" the hole by making it larger at the bottom than at the top; this provides a greater area for the patch to stick to.

2 INSTALL A BOLT AND CEMENT.

Hold the bolt in position and fill the hole with epoxy putty or anchoring cement. Make sure the bolt sticks up at the correct height, is plumb, and is in the correct position. Tamp the epoxy putty or cement firmly and meld it with the concrete surface.

ANCHOR THE TOP OF THE RAIL.

At the point where the rail meets the house, you need some serious fastening power. Small screws with plastic anchors will not hold. If the concrete has broken away, you will need to set bolts in cement or epoxy putty. Or fill the old hole and use a masonry screw or anchor. Masonry screws can be driven directly into pilot holes. Check the box to find the correct size of masonry bit to use. Drill the hole and drive in the screw.

You also can use masonry anchors, also called lag shields. Drill the correct-size hole (in some cases you can enlarge the old hole) and tap the anchor in until it is flush with the surface. Then hold the bracket in place and drive in the screw.

REPAIRING ASPHALT SURFACES

Asphalt, also called blacktop, is an inexpensive material with which to pave a driveway or a walkway. Because asphalt is made of gravel and petroleum tar rather than portland cement, it is flexible. It also is soft and requires regular maintenance. Every couple of years, you should seal asphalt surfaces with an emulsified sealer, sold in large buckets. Spread the sealer with a long-handled roller or squeegee made for the purpose. This seals small cracks before they get larger. If your asphalt is badly in need of maintenance, follow the steps here and on page 155 to fill potholes and cracks before applying sealer. If your driveway is too far gone for repair, call in a professional contractor to replace it; laying asphalt is not a do-it-yourself job.

YOU'LL NEED

TIME: A couple of hours for most patching jobs.

SKILLS: No special skills needed.

TOOLS: Small sledgehammer, masonry chisel, putty knife or trowel, shovel, tamper or piece of 4×4, roller or squeegee.

KEEP IT WARM

Asphalt is flexible when warm and brittle when cold. If possible wait for the temperature to reach at least 70°F before patching. If you must patch asphalt during cold weather, keep the materials and tools in a warm place until you use them.

Patching a pothole

1 DIG OUT THE HOLE AND ADD GRAVEL.

For a large damaged area, chip away loose asphalt and dig down about 12 inches or until you reach a solid base. Shovel in rocks and gravel to conserve patching material. Tamp down the gravel.

2 ADD ASPHALT AND TAMP.

Purchase bags of cold-mix asphalt patching compound and apply it in 1- to 2-inch layers. Slice the patching compound with your shovel to open any air pockets. Tamp down each layer firmly with the end of a 4×4 or a small tamper.

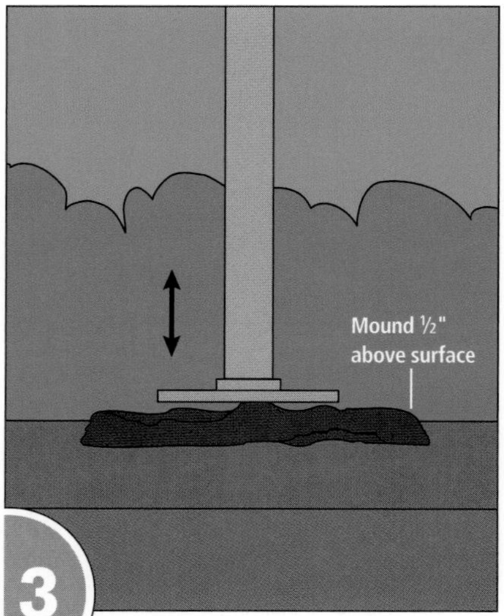

3 MOUND AND TAMP.

Keep adding and tamping patching compound until it is mounded about ½ inch above the surrounding surface. Tamp it firmly with a tamper. Sprinkle the patch with sand to prevent tracking, then drive a car back and forth over the patch to compact it until it is level.

4 SEAL THE AREA.

Seal the patch by pouring a generous amount of sealer on it and working it into the patch and the surrounding area. For the best results use a roller or a squeegee designed for sealing driveways. For small areas you can use a disposable paint roller. To achieve a uniform appearance, seal the whole driveway.

Patching a large crack

1 "KEY" THE CRACK.

For cracks wider than ⅛ inch, chisel away crumbling asphalt and "key" the hole, making the bottom wider than the top. Scrape and brush away loose debris. (Cracks narrower than ⅛ inch can be filled just with sealer.)

2 FILL WITH LIQUID FILLER.

Partially fill the crack with sand. Pour in liquid sealer or squeeze in asphalt sealer that comes in a caulking tube. Smooth out the patch with an old putty knife or trowel.

3 MIX AND APPLY PATCHING PASTE.

Mix sand with liquid sealer until you get a pastelike consistency. Push the paste into the crack with a trowel or putty knife, making sure to cram it into every corner. Smooth the patch so it is just above the surrounding surface.

REPAIRING BRICKS IN A PATIO

Patio bricks set in sand are easy to replace. The most difficult part of the job is removing the broken brick without damaging its neighbors.

If the patio bricks are mortared or set in concrete, use a masonry chisel and small sledgehammer to chisel out the damaged brick carefully, breaking and removing small pieces so you do not crack the surrounding bricks. Chisel away the mortar joints and concrete bed too. Brush latex bonding agent into the cavity and set the new brick in a bed of mortar.

YOU'LL NEED

TIME: About two hours to remove and replace bricks.

SKILLS: Care in removing damaged bricks.

TOOLS: Flat pry bar, hammer, masonry chisel, 4×4 for tamping.

1 REMOVE THE DAMAGED BRICK.

Use a flat pry bar to pry out the old brick. You may need to crack the brick and take it out in pieces. If it is a tight fit, try using two putty knives or trowels, one on each end, to shoehorn the brick straight up.

2 TAMP AND REPLACE.

Add sand and tamp the area well, making sure the sand level is not too high. Replace the brick and tap it level with a hammer and a piece of scrap wood. Fill the joints with fine sand, brush, and spray with water. Repeat until the sand remains at the level of the bricks.

GLOSSARY

For words not listed here, or for more about those that are, refer to the index, pages 158–160.

Aggregate. Gravel or crushed rock; when mixed with portland cement and water, it forms concrete.

Ashlar. Rectangular blocks of stone of uniform thickness used mainly to build dry walls.

Backfill. Soil used to fill in an excavation next to a wall. It adds stability to the wall and keeps water away from it.

Bat. A half-brick. Bats are used when whole bricks won't fit into the allotted space.

Batter. The practice of tapering the sides of a stone wall to give it added stability.

Batter board. A board frame supported by stakes set back from the corners of a structure. Saw kerfs or marks on the boards indicate the location of the edges of the footings and the structure, which can be used to reposition those points on the site following its excavation.

Bed joint. The horizontal layer of mortar between two courses of masonry units. See also Course.

Bond. (noun) Any one of several patterns in which masonry units can be arranged. (verb) To join two or more masonry units with mortar.

Brick set. A wide-blade chisel used for cutting bricks and concrete blocks.

Butter. To apply mortar on bricks or blocks with a trowel before laying them.

Cement. A powder that serves as the binding element in concrete and mortar.

Chink. A narrow piece or sliver of stone driven into cracks or voids in a stone wall to achieve added stability.

Closure brick (or block). The final unit laid in a course of bricks or blocks.

Concrete. A building and paving material made by mixing water with sand, gravel, and cement.

Concrete nails. Hardened-steel nails that can be driven into cured concrete.

Control joint. A groove tooled into a concrete slab during finishing to prevent random cracking later. To be effective these joints should be one-fourth the thickness of the slab.

Corner lead. The first few courses of masonry laid in stair-step fashion at a corner to establish levels for the remaining units in those courses.

Course. A row of masonry units. Most projects consist of several courses laid on top of each other and separated by mortar.

Darby. A long-blade wood float commonly used to smooth the surface of freshly poured concrete in situations where using a smaller float isn't practical.

Dry-laid wall. A wall of masonry units laid without mortar.

Edger. A concrete finishing tool for rounding and smoothing edges to strengthen them.

Efflorescence. A powdery stain, usually white, on the surface of or between masonry units. It is caused by the leaching of soluble salts from the mortar to the surface.

Expansion joint. The vertical space made in a concrete structure or between it and an existing structure to allow the concrete to expand and contract with temperature changes without damage to the surface.

Exposed-aggregate surface. A concrete finish achieved by embedding aggregate into a concrete surface.

Face brick. A type of brick made specifically for covering (veneering) walls.

Finish coat. The final coat of mortar or plaster in a stucco finish. See also Stucco.

Finishing. The final smoothing stage in concrete work.

Flashing. A layer of material, usually metal, inserted in masonry joints and attached to adjoining surfaces to seal out moisture.

Float. A rectangular wooden or metal hand tool used to smooth and compress wet concrete. Also the first process of finishing a concrete surface.

Footing. A thick concrete support for walls and other heavy structures built on firm soil and extending below the frost line.

Frost line. The maximum depth frost normally penetrates the soil during the winter. This depth varies from area to area depending on the climate.

Groover. A tool used for making control joints, or grooves, in concrete surfaces to control cracking. See also Control joint.

Grout. A thin mortar mixture. Also the process of applying grout. See also Mortar.

Head joint. The layer of mortar used to tie the ends of adjoining masonry units together.

Jointer. A tool used to finish the joints between masonry units. Joints are struck for aesthetic reasons as well as to compress the mortar into the joints.

Lead. See Corner lead.

Level. The condition that exists when a surface is at true horizontal. Also a tool used to determine level.

Masonry cement. A special mix of portland cement and hydrated lime used for preparing mortar. The lime adds to the workability of the mortar.

Modular spacing rule. A measuring device used to verify that a course of masonry units is at the proper height.

Mortar. A mixture of masonry cement, masonry sand, and water. For most jobs the proportion of cement to sand is 1 to 3. Also the process of applying mortar.

Nominal dimensions. The actual dimensions of a masonry unit, plus the thickness of the mortar joint on one end and at the top or bottom.

Plumb. The condition that exists when a surface is at true vertical.

Plumb bob. Tool used to align vertical points.

Pointing. See Tuckpointing.

Premix. Any of several packaged mixtures of ingredients used for preparing concrete or mortar.

Ready-mix. Concrete that is mixed in a truck as it is being transported to the job site.

Rebar (reinforcing rod). Textured steel rod used to reinforce concrete and masonry structures.

Reinforcing wire mesh. A steel screening used to reinforce certain types of concrete projects, such as walkways, drives, and patios.

Retaining wall. A wall constructed to hold soil in place.

Row-lock course. Several bricks laid side by side on their faces and pitched slightly (when used outdoors) to shed moisture; used below windows and as wall caps.

Rubble. Uncut stone found in fields or as it comes from a quarry. Often used for dry-laid walls.

Scratch coat. The first coat of mortar or plaster, roughened (scratched) so the next coat will stick to it.

Screed. A straightedge, often a 2×4 or 2×6, used to level concrete as it is poured into a form or to level the sand base in a form. Also the process of leveling concrete or a sand base.

Set. The process during which mortar or concrete hardens.

Slump. A measure of the wetness of a concrete or mortar mix; the wetter the mix, the more it spreads out, or slumps.

Spalling. Cracking or flaking that develops on a concrete surface or brick faces.

Square. The condition that exists when two surfaces are at 90 degrees to each other. Also a tool used to determine square.

Story pole. A measuring device, often a straight 2×4, with a series of marks set at regular intervals, used to verify that a course of masonry units is spaced at the proper height.

Straightedge. An improvised tool, usually a 1×4 or 2×4 with a straight edge, used to mark a straight line on material or to determine if a surface is even.

Stretcher. A brick or block laid between corner units.

Strike. The process of finishing a mortar joint. See also Jointer.

Stucco. A finish composed of two or more layers of mortar (white or colored) applied to either indoor or outdoor walls.

Throw mortar. To place mortar using a trowel.

Trowel. Any of several flat and oblong or flat and pointed metal tools used for handling and/or finishing concrete and mortar.

Tuckpointing. The process of refilling old masonry joints with new mortar.

Veneer. A layer of bricks or stones that serves as a facing.

Weep holes. Openings made in mortar joints to facilitate drainage of built-up water.

Whaler. A horizontal brace secured to the outside of a concrete form to strengthen it against the pressure of the concrete as it is poured.

Yard. A unit of volume in which ready-mix concrete is sold; equal to 1 cubic yard (27 cubic feet).

INDEX

Index *(continued)*

METRIC CONVERSIONS

U.S. Units to Metric Equivalents			Metric Units to U.S. Equivalents		
To convert from	Multiply by	To get	To convert from	Multiply by	To get
Inches	25.4	Millimeters	Millimeters	0.0394	Inches
Inches	2.54	Centimeters	Centimeters	0.3937	Inches
Feet	30.48	Centimeters	Centimeters	0.0328	Feet
Feet	.03048	Meters	Meters	3.2808	Feet
Yards	.9144	Meters	Meters	1.0936	Yards
Miles	1.6093	Kilometers	Kilometers	0.6214	Miles
Square inches	6.4516	Square centimeters	Square centimeters	0.1550	Square inches
Square feet	0.0929	Square meters	Square meters	10.764	Square feet
Square yards	0.8361	Square meters	Square meters	1.1960	Square yards
Acres	0.4047	Hectares	Hectares	2.4711	Acres
Square miles	2.5899	Square kilometers	Square kilometers	0.3861	Square miles
Cubic inches	16.387	Cubic centimeters	Cubic centimeters	0.0610	Cubic inches
Cubic feet	0.0283	Cubic meters	Cubic meters	35.315	Cubic feet
Cubic feet	28.316	Liters	Liters	0.0353	Cubic feet
Cubic yards	0.7646	Cubic meters	Cubic meters	1.038U	Cubic yards
Cubic yards	764.55	Liters	Liters	0.0013	Cubic yards

To convert from degrees Fahrenheit (F) to degrees Celsius (C), first subtract 32, then multiply by 5⁄9.

To convert from degrees Celsius to degrees Fahrenheit, multiply by 9⁄5, then add 32.